Still, I Rise

A Guide to Navigating the Caregiver Journey

Melody Vachal, M.S., CCC-SLP

Copyright © 2025 by Hummingbird Rising Press. All rights reserved.
ISBN 979-8-218-57151-1

Praise for Still, I Rise

"*Still, I Rise: A Guide to Navigating the Caregiver Journey* is an incredible resource for caregivers, written by someone who truly understands the journey from real-life experience. Melody offers practical suggestions illuminating the path through the often challenging caregiving landscape. Each chapter is filled with relatable anecdotes and actionable advice, making it a must-read for anyone stepping into the role of a caregiver.

With insightful strategies for managing stress and prioritizing self-care, this book empowers caregivers to provide the best care for their loved ones and nurture their own well-being. I wholeheartedly recommend this book to those seeking clarity and compassion in their caregiving experience."

—Vanessa Abraham M.S. CCC-SLP

"The unexpected trauma of having a loved one who needs care, along with the demands required, can overwhelm the caregiver physically, psychologically, and emotionally. Caregivers can become flooded with fatigue, sadness, anxiety, and feelings of loss. The ability to care for oneself can plummet. This book offers valuable guidance to help preserve the well-being of the caregiver, which is critical to preserving one's ability to provide care."

—John R. Lorenz, Ph.D., Licensed Clinical Psychologist and Family Therapist

"Melody Vachal has created a book that, through sharing the true story of her own loss and challenges, shows us the growth journey of caregiving. Vachal navigates difficult life circumstances for herself and her family with grit, positivity, and a nearly spiritual gift of acceptance. Her ability to surrender honestly to situations while remaining inspired and buoyant is a deep lesson here.

This tale also serves as an authoritative guide for those new to caregiving in the role of either provider or recipient. I read *Still, I Rise: A Guide to Navigating the Caregiver Journey* while adapting to the life-changing new reality of a very close friend who had been hit by a car, and it was immensely relevant. Vachal's suggestions make this book extraordinarily practical, and I credit it with helping me evolve into a more compassionate, supportive, and effective caregiver."

—Lori Doyle

"Many who face significant loss and health challenges often feel isolated in their struggles. *Still, I Rise: A Guide to Navigating the Caregiver Journey* is a testament to the human spirit's resilience. It shows that not only can one survive such ordeals, but they can truly RISE above them. With the support of a team, careful planning, and self-advocacy - as detailed in this book - individuals can transform their hardships into strength. The narrative doesn't dwell in despair; instead, it acknowledges the difficulties, celebrates the lessons learned, and offers hope. Melody Vachal stands as a beacon of resilience, ready to share her hard-earned wisdom with others who may be walking a similar path."

—Louise Shapiro, MSW

"It's amazing to see someone like Melody, who has faced every challenge life could throw at her, not only come through it all but also create a guide to help the rest of us. She brings such a unique perspective—not just as a caregiver but as someone who had to relearn life after a major accident. Let's be honest, no one would've blamed her if she chose to be persistently angry about it all, but instead, she came back stronger and with a mission to make sure caregivers feel seen and supported too. This book is practical, heartfelt, and a large dose of hope for anyone who's caring for someone or just wants to know how to support a caregiver friend."

—Jamie Jones, Family, and Psychiatric Nurse Practitioner

"As a Rehabilitation and Health Psychologist with extensive experience, supporting individuals with chronic medical conditions and disabilities and their caregivers, a guidebook such as this is an invaluable resource! Not only does it normalize the ups and downs of the caregiving experience, it provides great insights from the inside out. The reflective questions attached to each chapter are timely and relevant, and the direct tips for those who are in the trenches on a daily basis will support their physical health, mental health and overall wellness."

—Dr. Karen Golombecki, PsyD, LP

To my children and grandchildren,

Thank you for teaching me about unconditional love and inspiring me to rise in the face of life's challenges. This journey is for you, so you always know the power of resilience and the beauty of caring for one another.

And to all caregivers and care recipients,

May you find solace, strength, and a sense of purpose within these pages. Together, we rise.

Table of Contents

Prologue 5
Chapter 1: The Day Life Changed Forever 7
    Chapter 1: Chapter Questions and Workbook 15
Chapter 2: The Early Days of Caregiving 19
    Chapter 2: Chapter Questions and Workbook 31
Chapter 3: Building the Care Team 33
    Chapter 3: Chapter Questions and Workbook 47
Chapter 4: Caring for the Caregiver 49
    Chapter 4: Chapter Questions and Workbook 65
Chapter 5: Emotional and Psychological Impact of Caregiving . . . 67
    Chapter 5: Chapter Questions and Workbook 81
Chapter 6: Advocacy and Communication. 85
    Chapter 6: Chapter Questions and Workbook 99
Chapter 7: Small Victories and Milestones 103
    Chapter 7: Chapter Questions and Workbook 117
Chapter 8: Long-term Caregiving and Adaptation 119
    Chapter 8: Chapter Questions and Workbook 135
Chapter 9: Facing Challenges and Setbacks 139
    Chapter 9: Chapter Questions and Workbook 151
Chapter 10: The Road Ahead. 153
    Chapter 10: Chapter Questions and Workbook 163
Acknowledgements. 167

Prologue

I awoke in the middle of the night, unable to sleep. As I lay there in the quiet darkness, I kept hearing two words echo over and over in my mind: "rise up." They repeated with such clarity and insistence that I couldn't ignore them. Finally, I got out of bed and quietly left the room, drawn by the weight of those words, unsure of what they were calling me toward but knowing I needed to listen.

Sitting quietly, the words continued in my head, and I picked up my phone and, in the notes section, wrote:

"RISE UP exists to Refresh, Inspire, Support, Empower, Uplift, and Prepare caregivers for their caregiving journey."

I had just come to the point in my life where I understood what my journey was to be. I had been given a mission to move forward in healing myself and helping others. Through my experiences of being a caregiver and then as a recipient of care, it was now my turn to help others and to share my story. I had come full circle from caregiver to care recipient and now my calling was to use my knowledge and experiences to serve others.

I believe God had a plan for me and things are meant to be. Moving through all the challenges, chaos, and confusion of the care journey, I was to support others with my unique perspective of being on both sides of the care giving continuum. All I had been through was to teach me the importance of self-care, self-compassion, and support for others who walked through caregiving spaces. My healing gave me the opportunity to support and care for others in a new way.

There are an estimated 55 million family caregivers in the United States and the number is increasing as the baby boom generation ages. Whether you are an adult caring for aging parents, a parent caring for a child with physical, mental, or emotional needs, or a friend or neighbor who helps someone in need of care. You are providing essential services and support to someone in need. You may have entered the caregiving space willingly or been thrust into the world of caregiving. The journey may be one you had not even considered.

This book will give insight into a new world of caregiving and help you to understand and move forward in your caregiving journey. I hope and pray you will find it a guide to help you process your thoughts and experiences and help you persevere in the space of providing care. I want you to recognize and realize your value and the important role you play. I hope you will share it with friends and family to make their journey a bit lighter. It is the book I wish I had when I first entered the caregiving space - a guide to help me understand the profound changes happening in my life, many of which I didn't even recognize until I became a care receiver myself.

For so many years I had just been a "mom" caring for a child with special needs. It was what any mother would do, right? As a mother, you care for your children in whatever way you are called and support them throughout their lives. You are selfless and place their needs above your own. Even through all the challenges I had faced, from the moment I went to check on Isaac at daycare as a new mother and he was in acute respiratory arrest to the point a few hours later when he was airlifted from the hospital something significant had happened. I didn't realize it then, but something was different. The day Isaac's life changed from being a healthy baby to a child with life-altering disabilities, my life had also changed. I had started the day as a mother and within the span of a day, I had become a long-term caregiver.

"There are only four kinds of people in the world – those that have been caregivers, those that are caregivers, those who will be caregivers, and those who will need caregivers." — Rosalynn Carter

Watch Video:
Meet Melody:

http://www.melodyvachal.com/meet-melody

CHAPTER 1:
The Day Life Changed Forever

My day started out like any other day. I was getting ready for work, and Isaac, my 20-year-old son with disabilities, was being cared for by his caregiver, Lisa, who came every morning and helped him get ready for school. Shane, my 15-year-old, was also at home. It was just a regular spring day, one of those crisp, beautiful mornings in Minnesota when you can finally feel winter loosening its grip. I had been a caregiver for 20 years by that point – ever since Isaac's illness turned our world upside down and made caregiving my daily reality.

Isaac's journey began when he was just 10 weeks old. He had been a healthy, typical baby until one day when I called his daycare provider to check in. She said he hadn't eaten and seemed a little lethargic. He had only been in daycare for two weeks, and since I was still nursing, I figured I would stop by, feed him, and share a quick visit. But when I arrived a few brief minutes later, I found Isaac gray and struggling to breathe. I called an urgent care clinic and was told to get him to the emergency room immediately. My heart sank. My husband, who was nearby, arrived quickly and we sped to the ER, terrified of what might happen.

At the hospital, everything happened so fast. Isaac's blood glucose levels were through the roof and the doctors couldn't figure out what was wrong. He was in respiratory arrest and his temperature was down to 91.7. As we stood in anguish at the end of the gurney, all I could think about was that I might lose another child. Just one year before Isaac was born, I had given birth to my daughter, R.C., after seven and a half months' gestation. She lived for just 18 hours due to Trisomy 13, a condition that the doctors said was "incompatible with life." So, as I watched the doctors work frantically to save Isaac, all I could do was pray, "Please, just let him live. Whatever shape, whatever challenges he has, just let him survive." A helicopter arrived, and Isaac was airlifted to a larger hospital, where he spent weeks in the pediatric intensive care unit. The doctors feared the worst – a condition such as spinal muscular atrophy or a severe metabolic disorder – but Isaac held on.

Over time, we learned about his challenges: blindness, cerebral palsy, epilepsy, and cognitive and communication difficulties. My life as a caregiver really began then, balancing his needs with those of my other kids and the demands of my job as a speech-language pathologist. It wasn't easy, but we found our rhythm and life continued in that busy, exhausting way. Isaac needed constant care, and my caregiving role extended to my father as well. I was part of the "sandwich generation," caring for both my kids and an aging parent while trying to keep up with a full-time job. My marriage was also strained; my husband and I were living apart, trying to sort through our issues. Despite everything, I managed. Life was demanding, but it was the life I knew.

Then, on April 13, 2016, everything changed. I was preparing to leave the school where I worked as a speech therapist and had one more student to see at a nearby preschool program. I spent a few extra minutes with my students, frolicking on the playground and enjoying the beautiful spring weather before I loaded up my car to head to the preschool that was just a mile down the road. That's when a car accident turned my world upside down. I was stopped at a stoplight and suddenly there was a loud crash. A vehicle hauling a trailer smashed into my car, causing me to be propelled into two other vehicles in front of me. The next thing I remember is hearing the voice of the OnStar operator through the radio, asking if I was OK. All I could say was, "I can't feel my arms." She asked if I needed help, and I said yes, and asked her to make sure someone was taking care of Isaac and to notify my husband. My first thoughts weren't about myself, but about Isaac. Who would care for him if I couldn't? That's how it is when you're a caregiver – your first instinct is always concern for the person you're caring for.

The ambulance arrived and the paramedics placed a collar around my neck and removed me from the vehicle. My limp arm slipped off the gurney and they raised it back up next to my side and prepared to transport me to the hospital. As the paramedics strapped me to the gurney, I panicked. My heart was racing and even though I couldn't feel the straps, it was terrifying to be restrained and restricted, and I felt helpless. They rushed me to the hospital and in the ER, they ran tests – MRIs, CT scans – trying to figure out what was wrong. My husband, brother, and sister-in-law showed up, and we were all trying to wrap our heads around what was happening. I couldn't feel anything from my shoulders down, and all I could think was, "How can this be happening? Haven't I been through enough?" My fears and anxiety were overwhelming. As tears flowed from my eyes, others had to wipe them for me, and the realization hit me: this may be the rest of my life. I was in utter shock as I lay there, trying not to panic at what was happening.

Facing a New Reality

As they moved me to my hospital room, the reality of what I was facing really sank in. The nurses placed a bedpan under me, hoping I might be able to use it before they catheterized me. When I asked if I was done, they told me I had wet the bed, but I hadn't felt it happen. It was humiliating. I was filled with fear – fear for my future and for my family, and fear as I wondered how we would get through this. My marriage was already on shaky ground, and now I was facing the possibility of being completely dependent on others. The thought sent a wave of dread through me, a heavy realization that shook me to my core.

I realized I was on a new caregiving journey, but this time, I was the one who needed care.

While it wasn't discovered for a few days, the reality was that I had also sustained a traumatic brain injury in the accident. I knew I was struggling with serious symptoms, but I never imagined what it would be like to live life with a brain injury. I had always been a little scattered in my organizational skills, but my systems worked well enough for me. Nothing I had ever been through compared to this new reality. I felt disjointed and disconnected from my own body. Muscles and movements that had happened automatically before now needed great thought and effort. I had to think about the simplest of movements, and I felt like I was in a fog. Every sound, every light, and every action created a mind-numbing fatigue. My ears rang and all I wanted to do was go inside myself.

I longed for a silent, dark cocoon where there was no pain, light, or sound. The overwhelming emotions were beyond anything I could have imagined. I would burst into tears for no clear reason, and it literally felt like I was losing my grip on reality. I wanted so desperately to reverse the clock, to go back to the day of the accident and take a different route or wait just a few more minutes before I got in my car. That choice was not mine to make, and I had no choice but to live in this anguish. This was my new reality, and it was like a nightmare I couldn't wake up from.

My ability to focus was beyond me and concentration now required heroic efforts. I had been an extreme multitasker and now I struggled to follow even the simplest of directions. The smallest of tasks required intensive thought and effort which gave me a headache. I was dizzy and had double vision. My eyes were not working together and, as a result, I felt nauseous and like a stranger in my own body. Not only did my outside world seem different and dreamlike, but the inner world of my brain was not working. I struggled to understand and make sense of what I saw, heard, and felt. My attention and ability to engage were different. I couldn't make sense of what was happening around me. I felt like I had no purpose, and self-doubt overcame me as I tried earnestly to feel any sort of connection to my prior life.

While overwhelmed with a sense of desperation and the desire to decrease the stimulation and sensations that flooded through me, I thought about my students from past years. I imagined this might be what my students with autism felt like. I could understand why they would crawl under tables or behave in self-injurious ways. The sensations of this world could not be blocked or kept at bay. The outside world felt like it was attacking me at every turn. A space where I had thrived in managing so many tasks, and even enjoyed the busyness of life, was now a space I wanted to run or retreat from. I didn't know if I even wanted to be here anymore. I couldn't bear the thought of adding more to my family's plate. If this was my reality, was it worth it?

Not only did my body and brain feel like they were my enemies, but I was plagued with fear about the future. How could I possibly return to my old life? What was I good for anymore? I wasn't going to be able to provide the care my children needed. I certainly couldn't care for Isaac, and I could not imagine a world where I would be able to work in my chosen profession. In the span of seconds, the accident had changed and destroyed my life as I knew it. How could I possibly recover? I couldn't even fathom how things would ever get better, but I felt I had no choice other than to forge ahead through the pain and devastating new reality to start at square one. I had to continue. This was going to be the fight of my life.

The Challenge of Accepting Help

I've never been good at accepting help. Even in my childhood, I felt the need to be perfect. I set extremely high standards for myself and worked tirelessly to achieve them. While noticing that others needed help, I often sacrificed my own well-being to make life easier for others, I saw myself as a helper, carrying a sense of responsibility far beyond what my years should have required. This pattern of perfectionism didn't change when Isaac got sick. In fact, it intensified, and I felt if I didn't do everything correctly, Isaac wouldn't thrive.

Even when others offered or tried to help, I had to do it my way. It was my responsibility, and I took it seriously, perhaps too seriously at times. My own insecurities now surfaced with a vengeance, and I felt worthless and unnecessary. Now, not only could I not care for him, but I needed someone to take care of me. It was a hard reality to accept, but deep down I knew I had to push through the fear and focus on my recovery. I decided, even with the brain injury and paralysis, that I would give my recovery everything I had. I would approach it in the same way that I did when I cared for Isaac and when I moved through earlier challenges in my life; I decided my recovery would be my new job. I would do my best to become who I needed to be and who I had been for my family and, eventually, myself. I didn't want to be a burden to my family, and I wanted to keep being the mom my kids needed.

As I lay in the hospital bed everything was overwhelming - lights, sounds, emotions. My head throbbed and I felt like it would burst. When one of my friends, Merith, came to see me and fed me my meal, I couldn't quite believe this was reality. It just didn't seem possible, and I was scared this might be my new normal. How could I possibly be dependent on others when I was supposed to be the caregiver?

Being a caregiver is challenging, but accepting help can be even more challenging. You must find it within yourself as a care recipient to process through both the physical and emotional changes that come when you are the one in need of care. Never underestimate the importance of sharing your feelings about what you are going through. Access mental health services and let your caregivers know if you are struggling. This journey is not one most of us want to be a part of, even if we are grateful for the help. It is a humbling experience to be dependent on the care of others, so give yourself some grace as you adjust to the situation you are now in. Finding the opportunity to share your feelings and emotions is crucial for your well-being, both physically and emotionally. Take one day at a time as you allow yourself to adjust to changes and challenges. Realize every day that you are valuable whether you are giving or receiving care. Being both a caregiver and a care recipient gave me a whole new perspective.

I began to see the importance of open communication and not pushing away those who wanted to help.

I'd always been reluctant to let others assist with Isaac's care but now I had no choice. It became clear that having a dedicated support network was essential for both the caregiver and the person receiving care. I was blessed to have the support of my husband, family, and friends. Their support included checking in with doctors and therapists, managing the home front, coming to my hospital room and feeding me, keeping my spirits up, and praying for my healing and full recovery. I couldn't have had better teammates in the unexpected and unwanted journey I was about to begin.

Thinking back to being in that hospital bed, unable to move or feel, I knew I was facing another uphill battle. I realized that to recover and return to my role as a caregiver, I had to accept help, set boundaries, and take care of myself. This was a new chapter in my life, and I was determined to find the strength to rebuild and keep caring for the people I loved.

CHAPTER 1:
Chapter Questions and Workbook

Reflection Questions:

Thinking about your role as a caregiver, what are the biggest challenges you may face? What support do you need that you currently lack? How prepared do you feel to accept the role of a caregiver? How will you balance your needs with those of the care recipient? What could happen if something happens to you? Are you prepared for the unexpected?

Journal Prompts:

- What events led you to the role of caregiving?

_____

_____

_____

_____

_____

- How did you feel when you first realized you would be a caregiver? Describe your emotional and physical reactions.

_____

_____

- What were your initial thoughts and concerns? Have they changed?

- How have you been managing and reflecting on this journey with your care recipient?

Action Steps:

As a caregiver, take the opportunity to complete the following stress assessment. For each question, rate from 1 meaning "never" to 10 meaning "all the time". Feel free to jot specific notes as reminders of how you are feeling at this point. We will do this assessment again at the end of the book to see what, if anything, has changed in your viewpoint.

Pre-Test

Question	Rating (1-10)	Notes
How often do you feel overwhelmed by caregiving?		
How are you balancing your caregiving duties with other aspects of your life (e.g. work, personal time)?		
How often do you find yourself physically exhausted due to caregiving?		
How often do you find time for yourself for self-care or activities that help you relax?		
How frequently do you experience feelings of guilt related to caregiving?		
How often do you feel emotionally drained by caregiving?		
How well do you think you manage stress when unexpected caregiving challenges occur?		
How frequently do you experience loneliness or isolation as a caregiver?		
How supported do you feel (by friends, family, community resources) in your caregiving role?		
How confident are you in your ability to continue in your caregiving role without significantly impacting your own health?		

It is important to prepare in case the day comes when you are the one needing care.

1. Start to think about creating or revisiting your emergency plan.

2. Make sure you have a clear plan in place in case something happens.

3. Name the people who can be available to help you in case of emergency and make sure they know their roles. To determine what roles and needs are required in an emergency, look at the care recipient's medical conditions, daily living needs, and any health risks. This will help you decide who is the best option to handle specific tasks such as medical decisions, financial responsibilities and care coordination.

4. List out the key people in your support network. Talk to them about your needs and how they can help. Take the opportunity before a need is at hand to bring your team on board with you. This will alleviate some of the stress if extra help is needed.

5. It is also important to designate a healthcare power of attorney who can help make decisions for you if you are unable to do so. Having a healthcare directive completed so your wishes are known and understood in the event you are unable to state your wants and needs yourself is also of vital importance. You can request a healthcare directive from your medical provider, hospitals, or legal professionals. Some states also offer online templates or forms on government websites.

By reflecting on these questions, journaling your thoughts, and taking proactive steps, you can better navigate challenges and build a stronger support system for your recovery.

*"Our greatest glory is not in never falling,
but in rising every time we fall."* — Confucius

CHAPTER 2:
The Early Days of Caregiving

Little did I know the challenges that lay ahead on the first day after the accident. Thankfully, I was beginning to have a pins and needles sensation in my body, which gave me at least some hope that I was not going to be paralyzed forever. Even so, my body was not my own. I needed help to eat, roll over, and attend to all my personal care. As I lay motionless in my hospital bed, my heart kept going back to Isaac and I wondered how I would be able to care for him. How would the rest of my family pick up the slack? What did this mean, not only for my life, but theirs as well?

I knew there were many obstacles ahead but at this point, all I could do was desperately try to stay in the moment, even though it was a terrifying space. I was always the person who helped others and now I was helpless. I had never imagined this reality. It had never crossed my mind that I would need the care of others when I had still been so capable just the day before.

One thing I knew was that I didn't give up easily. I had already lived through the death of my newborn daughter and the loss of Isaac's health and normal development. My parents had shown perseverance and the importance of hard work, and my faith sustained me through earlier challenges. I just had to believe it would sustain me again or I didn't know how else I could move forward.

I was grateful I had the support of my spouse, family, and friends but I wasn't sure what that would look like in the days and perhaps months or years of recovery. I was not used to having people care for me in the way that had quickly become a necessity. I felt overwhelmed and afraid, but I didn't want to let it show. I wanted to keep up the same positive attitude that had sustained me through other challenges, but I think I was simply in denial regarding the road I had to face.

A Devastating Conversation with a Neurosurgeon

I remember the day after the accident. I was lying in bed and my husband was there. The neurosurgeon came in to check on me to see if there was any change in my condition. I was feeling hopeful because I had started to have sensation and could ever so slightly move my fingers. I was hoping he would be encouraging and give me a sense of success and hope. Instead, he shook his head and very abruptly told me, "That's nothing," and asked, "Is that the only change?" To hear this disregard and almost contempt from a doctor was a tough pill to swallow and I felt incredibly defeated. I was trying desperately to have something to cling to and he came in and, in a moment, all the hope I had was gone.

This was the first lesson I learned on my journey – find a doctor you trust and believe in! On this day, my husband left the room and made sure that the doctor never returned.

It is crucial to surround yourself with a team of people who believe in you and whom you can trust implicitly.

In addition, having people in your corner who support you when you are unable to manage is a gift that cannot be underestimated. I had always felt that I was the person who was a support for others, and I struggled mightily with accepting help and kindness for myself.

Lesson number two: When people offer help, they do so because they want to help and not out of obligation. Allowing others to care for you is a gift for yourself and it helps them as well. It allows people to feel less helpless and lets them share the love and compassion they have for you. Even though it was incredibly humbling, I had no choice but to accept care and compassion from both loved ones and strangers.

Because my spinal cord was intact, the medical staff believed swelling was causing the paralysis. They gave me medications to bring down the swelling and, thankfully, we began to see some changes over the next few days. I don't think I fully understood what my journey was going to entail. Even though I had worked in rehabilitation as my career, I had no idea what was to come on the journey I was about to embark upon.

My First Step on the Road to Recovery

The days after the accident were a whirlwind as medical professionals – including doctors, nurses, physical therapists, occupational therapists, and speech therapists – came in and put me through the first paces of what would become years of therapy. Each one came with their tests and measurements, and being a person who always wanted to excel, I tried desperately to complete the tasks they presented.

I knew that I was failing, and it was devastating to me at this point in my life. I couldn't do what I had always done and simply succeed. Not only did I not succeed but I also felt like a failure. Maybe if I tried harder, listened more carefully, or dug deeper, I could do the things they asked.

At this point in my life, I was 52 years old, and I had the physical development of a newborn. I needed help with everything. I wasn't sure if I would ever have more skills than I did at that time. In addition to the physical movement challenges, I had a traumatic brain injury. My head pounded and the lights and sounds of the hospital overwhelmed me. I felt foggy and had difficulty understanding and processing information.

I thought back to the time when my son, Isaac, first got sick and we entered the pediatric intensive care unit and saw the other shell-shocked parents in the waiting area. I felt so incredibly overwhelmed.

It was strange how in that situation I acclimated sooner than I thought I would. Within days, I was chatting around the coffee machine like an "old timer" and discussing things like O^2 saturation levels and test results. I remember watching the "newbies" come in, scared stiff at what they were facing.

Now I only hoped I could become more comfortable with being a patient versus a caregiver. It felt like I had entered a foreign country in many ways. I didn't know it then but the journey this time, with me needing care, would require much more effort on my part.

The Mental Transition from Caregiver to Care Recipient

I had been a caregiver, and I understood that world and felt comfortable in it. I had lived caregiving for 20 years, but I thought to myself, "How am I ever going to understand and accept the journey where I am the person in need of care? I am the one who gives care, not receives it!"

For years, I had been a caregiver. I was extremely comfortable caring for both my son and my father, and I understood many tips and tricks which made that world navigable. Being able to accept care was something I was not prepared for, and I didn't want it. I wanted to be the one who was doing the caring and not receiving the care.

It is sometimes a blessing that we don't know the steps of our journey before they occur, but it can be important to have some thoughts and conversations about the "what ifs." My hope is for no one to ever have these types of experiences, but it is better to have "think ahead" moments just in case. Take the time to have conversations about whom you can rely on and count on if things get tough. Who do you know that you could ask for help on a moment's notice?

We never know when a split-second can change an entire life. I certainly had never imagined my life at this point. I felt challenged as I tried to focus on myself and dig deep when my normal MO was to focus on everyone else. I had to do my best because others counted on me for their care. I had to recover for myself and for everyone who needed and depended on me.

Later in the day, one of the physical therapists who had seen me earlier came back to my room. He said he had thought about me during the day and had a little extra time before his shift ended, and he wanted to get me sitting up. I was scared but hopeful that we could make some progress. The medication had been helping and I was experiencing more sensations in my body. I was willing to accept the help he offered.

Slowly, we worked my body into a seated position, and I shook like a leaf. My body was not well integrated, and all my nerve functions were going haywire. He helped me sit upright on the bed, with my legs hanging over the side. I must have looked like a shivering, twitching mass of a person. Even though I couldn't sit unassisted, I was upright, and I dug deep and tried my hardest. As I sat on the side of the bed, my legs shook uncontrollably but it was a start. I had a journey to recover and now was the time to begin.

My parents had taught me to always do my best and I clung to that in these difficult moments. My dad used to say it didn't matter whether you were paid 50 cents or $5.00, you should work just as hard on the job. I took that as a challenge and vowed that I would treat my recovery like a job. I was going to do everything I possibly could to get back to "normal" in whatever way possible. I had no idea what challenges lay before me and how long my journey would last. All I knew was that people depended on me, and it was my duty to move forward.

Inpatient Rehabilitation Begins

The next day, Dr. Kelly Collins joined my care team, and she turned out to be a true blessing. A physiatrist specializing in physical medicine and rehabilitation, she was admitting me to the inpatient rehabilitation program when I met her. I felt an instant connection with her and was so relieved to have a physician of her caliber and ability. She had a completely different demeanor from the neurosurgeon, and I felt so comfortable with her. This was one of the first bright spots I had experienced since the accident.

She spoke in a manner which showed her knowledge and compassion and made me feel incredibly at ease. I didn't know it then, but we were going to be spending time together for the next several years as I recovered. It was probably good that, at the time, I did not know how long it was going to take to recover. However, I can say now that I couldn't have had a better doctor alongside me on my journey to return to myself.

Having people on your team is one particularly important way to work through the caregiving journey and I'm so grateful this doctor was with me on my journey. As I transitioned into inpatient rehabilitation, I met so many wonderful therapists, nurses, and patient care attendants. I worked as hard as I could to complete the tasks they asked. It was an exhausting and mind-numbing journey to have therapy after therapy. Each time I completed a session, I couldn't wait to get back to my bed and reset. The level of fatigue and exhaustion was unlike anything I'd ever experienced. I had never known such challenging and important work outside of being a caregiver myself.

The ability of these professionals reminded me once again of the importance of a care team. Having experts involved in my care was an absolute necessity if I had any hope of recovery. I had spent years developing the same thing for Isaac, but now the focus was on me.

The Importance of Support for Caregivers and Care Recipients

I felt like I was constantly struggling to keep the gas in my tank. It seemed to always sit just slightly above empty, and it took all I had to keep going. There was a new understanding of the importance of conserving energy. I had an all-or-nothing type of personality, and I had never been good at pacing. It was a struggle every day to be unable to easily do simple tasks like dressing and feeding myself. I had never known this level of fatigue and overwhelm. My therapists suggested ideas for minimizing the fatigue that were new to me. Things that seemed silly to me, like only making one trip to gather items, or putting all my clothes on my walker before I returned to my bed to dress, proved invaluable as I needed all my energy to complete daily tasks and therapy.

It made me begin to understand the importance of supporting not only caregivers, but those who have to receive care. Neither is an easy road and they both need grace and encouragement as well as incredible empathy. I couldn't have done it without the support of family, friends, professionals, my faith, and my belief that God had a plan for my life.

Accepting help from others came with a steep learning curve for me. It was humbling and I was not altogether comfortable with being on the receiving end of care.

Heading Home for Outpatient Therapy

After a few weeks of this intensive rehabilitation, it was time to transition back to my home where I would continue my recovery in outpatient rehabilitation. I progressed to using a walker and could move about my environment independently, but I still needed someone there to support me and provide care. I was anxious to return home and be reunited with my family. I knew I would still need assistance from someone else to get to my therapy appointments and to manage household tasks that I was unable to perform. Thankfully, we could easily find a caregiver. My husband had started a home care company to provide care for Isaac when our son was an infant, and we were able to have a caregiver come into the home. Now I had a caregiver who had to help me with everything – showering, meals, and household tasks. She was also able to provide care for me and take me to all my therapy appointments. I would be in outpatient rehabilitation for several years as I continued to heal my broken body and broken brain.

The role reversal was tough. Watching my caregiver, I realized how much I'd underestimated the importance of self-care for caregivers. I saw how hard she was working and how crucial it was for her to take breaks, something I'd rarely allowed myself. I was so grateful to have her help even while I felt embarrassed about needing it. I was supposed to be "doing" and it was incredibly difficult to adjust from being necessary and helpful to just "being." I was good at doing, caring for others, and keeping all the balls in the air, and now I had to learn to receive. It was one of the hardest things I have ever done, and I will never again underestimate the role of caregivers providing service and support.

As I watched her, I learned so much more than I had ever known about caregiving from the outside looking in. In fact, it was while watching my caregiver that I first began to really understand all I had done to care for others and that I, too, was a caregiver.

You see, I had not conceptualized that I was a caregiver. Even though I had been a caregiver for two decades, I still thought of myself in relationship to the person for whom I was providing care. I was doing what you did for family. It didn't mean I was a caregiver. I was a daughter as well as the mother of three children. That is what family means. Not realizing this earlier had kept me from understanding the true level of commitment involved in being a caregiver. I had been a "sandwich generation" caregiver, but it took me being cared for by another to realize the importance of the role I had played.

This is something I notice now in my work with caregivers.

All too often we simply identify ourselves through our relationship with those we care for. We don't prioritize ourselves as caregivers.

I certainly did not. It took me watching my caregiver and thinking, "She is really doing a lot of work" or "Maybe she should take a break." I wondered how she had the energy to do everything she was doing for me on top of the roles she played in her own life. Watching her care for me was truly an epiphany. In fact, it came to me in the middle of the night a few months after my accident.

I awoke in the middle of the night, unable to sleep. As I lay there in the quiet darkness, I kept hearing two words echo over and over in my mind: "rise up." They repeated with such clarity and insistence that I couldn't ignore them. Finally, I got out of bed and quietly left the room, drawn by the weight of those words, unsure of what they were calling me toward but knowing I needed to listen.

Sitting quietly, the words continued in my head, and I picked up my phone and, in the notes section, wrote:

"RISE UP exists to Refresh, Inspire, Support, Empower, Uplift, and Prepare caregivers for their caregiving journey."

I had just come to the point in my life where I understood what my journey was to be. I had been given a mission to move forward in healing myself and helping others. Through my experiences of being a caregiver and then as a recipient of care, it was now my turn to help others and to share my story. I had come full circle from caregiver to care recipient and now my calling was to use my knowledge and experiences to serve others.

I believe God had a plan for me and things are meant to be. Moving through all the challenges, chaos, and confusion of the care journey, I was to support others with my unique perspective of being on both sides of the care giving continuum. All I had been through was to teach me the importance of self-care, self-compassion, and support for others who walked through caregiving spaces. My healing gave me the opportunity to support and care for others in a new way.

A Starting Point in My Identity as a Caregiver

My journey had been a starting point to serve others. My experiences were challenges that could help other caregivers and families. Every day, caregivers show up in spaces and ways that they didn't know were possible. They may not have any idea about how they are to navigate the new world they have entered.

They may not understand the importance of their role and may be reluctant to assume it. In fact, it often feels like you are trying to take a test you didn't study for. There are unfamiliar terms and conditions to assume and implement. It is often a space of moving from being overwhelmed to calm, from chaos to organization, and from feeling alone to accessing support.

Allowing yourself to stay calm reduces anxiety and helps manage the feeling of being overwhelmed, which is often the hallmark of the first stages of caregiving. Staying organized provides a sense of control which lowers stress. Sharing your burden and your journey with others reduces anxiety and decreases the sense of isolation that is often present when you are a caregiver. I had decades of practice in caring for others and now I needed to use the tools to care for and heal myself.

I certainly had struggled with calm and serenity during my caregiving journey. New realizations came to me as I healed. My brain injury forced me into spaces of calm and quiet. I would return from therapy and need to have a peaceful space to recover and reset. My go-to was earplugs, an eye mask, and a weighted blanket in the beginning. Over time, I worked to use different tools like mindfulness and meditation to find my calm.

Feeling overwhelmed is a main feature of a brain injury and I struggled with it daily. For apparently no reason at all, I would burst into tears and become very fearful and uncertain. It took a long time to find calm in my life, and it is a practice I am still working on refining. Calmness allows me to respond more effectively to changing situations and keeps things stable in the environment. It did not come naturally to me, but I knew I could learn new skills and ways to manage a journey I had never wished for.

The more organized you are as a caregiver, the more consistent you can be. In fact, I learned from a friend that consistency is key. Intensity needed to be managed with my brain injury, and this is also true for caregiving. An all-or-nothing approach can send you spinning and make it difficult to accomplish anything. Everyone has their own style – what is yours?

Before my accident, I called my style of organization "organized chaos." I had to move into a fresh style of organization, and it was incredibly challenging. I understood now that my standard operating system had to be revamped, and it started with how I coordinated and organized my own recovery.

I had notebooks and folders of activities, tasks, and challenges for myself. I researched ways to help me understand my new normal and I slowly allowed myself to rely on others as I never had before. In fact, if I had been aware of more of these things earlier in my journey, perhaps my life would have been different. I might have been able to be a better partner if I had been able to communicate my fears, needs, and hopes. I held on to everything as if my life depended on it. Perhaps my marriage might have survived in spite of all the trauma we sustained as a couple and a family. I can only speculate now on the differences life may have held if I could have released my tight grip and let go. Looking back can provide a perspective that we don't always recognize in the moment.

Due to the higher risk of burnout that is prevalent with untreated stress, better health outcomes for a caregiver will happen if calmness is present.

Being organized helps to maintain balance between caregiving and all the other aspects of your life. Balance is the key to wellness for caregivers.

Allowing others to support you and learning to support yourself are basic building blocks which can be used repeatedly in the caregiving journey. So now let's explore ways to approach the caregiving journey with an openness to learning, growing, and realizing the best possible outcomes for both caregivers and care recipients.

CHAPTER 2:
Chapter Questions and Workbook

Reflection Questions:

Do you view yourself as a caregiver and how has that impacted your relationship with the one you care for? How are you allowing others to support you and are you able to share the load? What strategies did you use to cope with the initial stages of shock and being overwhelmed? Were these strategies effective? What do you identify as your current needs? What is your organizational style?

Journal Prompts:

- When faced with challenges, how do you typically navigate through them, and what have you learned about your strengths and needs as a result?

_____

_____

_____

_____

- What is currently causing you the most stress? How are you managing your stress levels?

_____

_____

_____

_____

- Are there additional strategies or skills you're interested in developing to support your growth? How might these new tools help you in your caregiving journey?

_____

_____

_____

_____

Action Steps:

Dedicate 5-10 minutes each day to developing practices that will calm your mind and your body. These may be meditation, prayer, or a quick walk outdoors. Including them in your daily routine or setting a reminder on your phone allows you the opportunity to consciously relax during the day. It is essential to begin to prioritize yourself as you care for others.

Another opportunity for growth is to take an inventory of the spaces and tools you use for care. When you have an organized space and know where the supplies and documents are for care needs, it reduces the time you spend searching for them. This will help you to conserve both your time and energy – both are essential for your own well-being.

"I can do things you cannot, you can do things I cannot, together we can do great things." — Mother Teresa

CHAPTER 3:
Building the Care Team

When Isaac first began to receive special education services, he was only 16 weeks old. In our state, we had something called an Individual Family Service Plan, which helped to pull together a team of people who might be helpful for children with special needs and their families. The three departments involved were Education, Health, and Human Services. This plan helped us to figure out which supports were available and who might be able to partner with us for Isaac's particular needs. As he got older, this switched to an individual education plan (IEP), which is developed through the school system for educating students requiring special education.

You may also find these teams within medical settings. There may be a healthcare case manager or a medical social worker who facilitates these teams. In this chapter, we will discuss how you can build your own team to support you and your loved one.

Find the Right Providers

In our last chapter, we touched on two important lessons. One, find a doctor who communicates effectively and whom you can trust and respect. Two, accept help when help is offered. Both can be challenging because as caregivers we may not recognize the importance of our voice and our needs. This is where the team can be of great benefit.

Having a physician or primary care provider who recognizes you as the expert in your own story is essential. Trust yourself enough to know whether something does not feel right or equal in this particularly important collaborative relationship. I have been fortunate in my journey to have collaborated with amazing physicians, not only for my care but also for the care of my son.

A key takeaway that helped me was to realize that there are many providers, and each has a different personality, style, and perspective. Finding your alignment helps make the process and the ongoing care so much easier. And do not forget that they are there for you. If you are not feeling a connection or value in the relationship and care, it may be time to find another provider. Sometimes, although a medical professional's bedside manner is lacking, you recognize the skill and depth of knowledge and are willing to take the tradeoff. Everyone has their own style and things that matter to them. Trust yourself and your judgment.

Accepting help is difficult for many of us in the caregiving space. We operate on the powerful sense of duty and responsibility we feel we have toward our loved ones and those we care for.

I believed if I did not manage everything myself, then I would be responsible for the outcome.

For example, with Isaac I thought if I personally did not do all the exercises, the therapy, and every potential step in the journey it would be my fault if he did not overcome his challenges. Fear can far surpass our rational minds. There is a reason fear has been referred to as **F**alse **E**vidence **A**ppearing **R**eal. I believed he would never reach his full potential if I did not "do it right." Now I realize the tremendous pressure I was putting on an already demanding experience. You are not an island and the best time to realize that is at the very beginning of the journey.

Learning to Let Go and Let Others

There is also a loss of control over how care looks when it is provided by someone other than you and this can be anxiety-producing for caregivers who are used to managing every aspect of the caregiving process. I struggled to trust that others could have the same level of commitment and care. My own anxiety did not allow me to ask others for help. Guilt about being a burden to others or the belief that as a caregiver you are supposed to be able to oversee everything on your own can be a difficult space to navigate.

Quite honestly, a lack of awareness of the load you carry, or knowledge of options can be a stopping point to accessing help as well. Distinct cultural norms and societal expectations can also play a significant role in beliefs about accepting help from others. Understanding roadblocks to accessing support can help caregivers recognize the need for helping hands and accept the help more easily.

As you move forward, taking these first two lessons to heart, it is crucial to develop a dream team to achieve the best possible outcomes. It is essential to find and recruit the absolute best medical professionals, therapists, and support staff to accompany you on your journey.

Building Your Team

There are any number of people who can join your team. Your only limitations are your choices and who you believe can best offer you the support and skill set for your needs. Family and friends can also be a part of your team. One thing to remember as you begin to construct your team is the importance of setting up ground rules and boundaries. This can be especially true in the realm of family and friends.

While we all experience moments of gratitude, there can be times when it feels like others are trying to step in and drive the bus. There also may be people we love whom we do not necessarily want on our team. I struggled with boundaries and sticking with them as a day-to-day caregiver.

***Let's face it, family is not always helpful
even if they have the best of intentions.***

I remember my mother saying repeatedly about my son, Isaac, "If only he could see, then he could… (fill in the blank here)."

There were so many options. It was so difficult to hear as I had agonized over these same feelings myself. I know they came from a place of deep love and sorrow when any of my mother's grandchildren or children were suffering with pain or loss. Rather than setting a boundary of asking her not to say it anymore because it was hard to hear, I finally just blew up one day and said forcefully, "Well he can't and he's never going to," and I started to cry. She felt awful and so did I.

This could have easily been remedied and addressed if I had simply asked in a calm state that we not talk about "what if" or "if only." Instead, I felt terrible and so did she. Remember to think ahead about the boundaries and limits you need related to your team.

This is a time when consulting with the person receiving care is important if it is possible. While he or she may not necessarily want added care providers, it is necessary for your health and well-being as the primary caregiver. I have spoken with countless families over the years who needed additional care, and the care recipient was not in favor. While the care recipient's opinion also matters, being able to set up boundaries around your need for breaks and self-care as the primary caregiver will allow you the space to advocate for your needs. You also want to think of the members of your team – why you want them, how they may show up, and when it might be helpful to have them available.

No one tells you how challenging the journey of caregiving is or how to prepare yourself. You do not necessarily know the steps you can take to make your load lighter. Taking the time early in the journey to develop your care team is worth the effort. Know, too, that your team will inevitably change. There is a well-known quote by Brian A. "Drew" Chalker, that says, "Some people come into your life for a reason, some for a season, or some for a lifetime." This is true for care teams as well.

You may have people on your team who make sense if you are caring for a child but may not continue as that child ages. There may be friends who are there for you at the beginning, but they may phase out of your life because your journeys no longer align. This can be painful but thinking ahead of the long road may help. Remember, everyone's journey has a different number of steps. Sometimes people are only meant to go with you on parts of the road. You will grieve the loss of team members and stages of the journey and that is normal.

Ripples of Care

When building a care team, I like to think of the "ripples of care." If you imagine a pond or a lake into which a stone is thrown, you see ever-widening ripples in the water which spread out from the center. Where the stone hits the water, you have the epicenter of the first ripple. This signifies the care recipient. He or she is the first ripple because everything eventually comes back to them. They are the reason we form a team to begin with. If they are able, the care recipient should be an active participant in the care team selection and can lead along with the primary caregiver.

I know there were times during my recovery when things were difficult to deal with, yet I still wanted to be the active voice of my own needs. Focusing on the center of the circle allows us to view the interconnectedness of care surrounding the care recipient and its flow into an ever-widening circle of support. It is challenging for both the care recipient and the primary caregiver which is why it is best to have both involved in the process.

Our first ripple is the primary caregiver. They are often the leader of the care team or share the role with the care recipient. As the leader they must become comfortable with asserting and advocating for their needs as well as setting up the best standard of care.

Our second ripple is the secondary caregivers. They may be family, friends, or hired caregivers who support the care recipient and the primary caregiver. Take the time to do your research to discover who might make the best secondary caregivers for your team. It can be helpful to think ahead to what your expectations are of this person or people.

1. Do you need them to be regular caregivers or are they only needed in emergency situations?
2. Are you able to find enough secondary caregivers so you can continue to have a sense of the life you led before caregiving?

I had caregivers for myself, and we had secondary caregivers come in and care for my son while I was recovering and throughout his entire journey. If not for secondary caregivers, I would not have been able to work my job as a speech-language pathologist. Secondary caregivers would come to our home before school to prepare my son for his day and, at the end of the day, care for him until I returned from work.

Eventually, we had secondary caregivers into the early evening. Having these folks on our care team allowed my younger son to take part in activities which would not have been possible if I were having to provide all the care myself. Just a reminder here that secondary caregivers can allow you space for self-care and time away from day-to-day caregiving.

Do not underestimate the importance of having help with caring for your loved one. You may find that you ebb and flow between primary and secondary caregiving. After my accident, I was unable to function as a primary caregiver. I had to take a step back and for a period of time became a secondary caregiver. Eventually I flowed back into primary caregiving. Just as water is fluid, so is caregiving and it is essential not to lock yourself into one category.

Allowing others to assist you in caregiving is crucial to avoid the burnout often noted in caregiving circles.

The final ripple of care on our care team consists of community support. This may include friends, neighbors, home healthcare staff, public health representatives, service groups, faith communities, doctors, school staff, nurses, therapists, nutritionists, pharmacists, pain management facilitators, attorneys, financial planners, social workers, and mental health or medical specialists.

Conducting a Needs Assessment

To determine who should be an addition to your care team, it is helpful to assess the needs and care requirements of the person in need. This can include medical, emotional, and daily care needs. A needs assessment allows you to understand the care recipient's baseline and the specific requirements of care. To conduct the needs assessment, you will want to know the following information:

1. What are the current medical needs? This can include a review of the individual's medical history, diagnoses, medications, and treatment.

2. What has been successful and what are the upcoming needs for specific treatment protocols? Figuring out upcoming appointments and transportation needs can be helpful as you are planning for care as well. This is especially important if you are relying on a care team member to support you in this area.

3. Are there any current unmet needs for specialists or special medical care?

4. What needs have been assessed related to assistive devices

including durable medical equipment such as walkers, wheelchairs, hospital beds, or home modifications?

5. What daily needs need to be considered? Daily needs may include personal care, nutrition, mobility, and household duties. Looking at daily needs for personal care such as dressing, eating, grooming, and toileting gives you a sense of how much added support you may need going forward.

6. Added support may be necessary for nutrition and dietary needs such as specific diets, feeding help, or meal preparation.

7. What help is necessary for moving around the environment, transfers, and fall prevention?

8. What extra support do you need as a caregiver to complete household duties such as laundry, cleaning, grocery shopping, or home maintenance?

Emotional and Social Needs to Consider

The emotional and social needs of both the care recipient and caregiver are significant. Notable things to consider are how the care recipient is dealing with the changes in their life. Having the ability to evaluate emotional well-being and potential mental health concerns should not be underestimated. Life changes related to the loss of independence were also difficult as I recovered, and I am grateful that my care team supported not only my physical health but also my mental health.

Changes also occurred related to social interactions and community engagement. As a person living with a brain injury, my social situation changed overnight. I had always enjoyed large groups and received my energy and feedback from my communication and engagement with others. I thrived in these social environments and enjoyed the opportunity to be around my friends and family.

After the accident I no longer had the bandwidth to be in groups. There was too much chaos, overstimulation, and it was simply too exhausting to manage. I still had a need for connection, but it needed to be in small doses with limited people. Even today, as I navigate groups, I often need a recovery period after time in noisy or large group settings.

Connection is still important to me, but it is necessary to alter how it looks now compared to before my brain injury. You might notice similar changes with your loved ones. It's also essential to consider existing support networks, such as family, friends, and other resources.

Financial Needs

Financial planning is an essential aspect of the needs assessment process. Taking the time to review current financial resources and limitations along with savings, costs of care, and insurance coverage can be useful as you figure out whether the care recipient is eligible for any government assistance or financial aid. Having the opportunity to sit down with a financial adviser is helpful as you look at the long-term costs of care and how they may impact you now and in the future. Information is power in these situations.

Emergency Plan Needs

Finally, having an emergency plan in place for you and your care recipient is helpful. When my accident occurred, we had never discussed emergency plans. At the very least you should have a list of emergency contacts and people you can quickly access if needed. Also think about what happens in times of natural disaster. This might be things like evacuation plans or backup generators if your loved one has significant medical needs and conditions. Ensuring that you have thought through and addressed these items in your needs assessment is vital for your well-being as well as that of your loved ones.

Develop Your Care Team

When you have completed your needs assessment through gathering information from your care providers and family members, the care recipient and primary caregiver can use this information to shape the development of your care team. This will ensure that all aspects of care are addressed effectively and efficiently.

Once your assessment of needs is complete, you will not only be able to define and outline the roles and responsibilities of the care team, but you should also select the right people for the job.

It is important to choose people with whom you feel comfortable. You want folks on board who have not only the skills but also the experience to move forward with you on your journey. Temperament and personality should also be considerations. Do not feel like you are stuck in any situation or with specific team members. You must be willing to seek out the team you need for now. You can make replacements at any time or draft new team members. It is a little like being a team coach. You know what the best outcome will be for your loved one.

If you find you need help, you have a team with a variety of skills and talents. Utilize it to best support you and the one you care for. Trust yourself and your team. If you are unsure or need help, look to your trusted friends, family, and team members.

Ask for recommendations from people who are in similar situations. Do your research and remember you are in the driver's seat. You get to choose your providers and, if someone does not feel like a good fit, do not be afraid to keep looking for the right person. Ask yourself these questions:

1. Who are you most comfortable with?
2. What personality types fit with your style of communication and desired personal interaction?

3. Are you willing to have a great provider for whom you may not necessarily have warm, fuzzy feelings?
4. Can I collaborate with these people for the best possible results for my loved one? If the answer is yes, you are on the right path.

These are all questions to ask yourself and research as your team continues to grow and evolve. Remember to trust yourself and your judgment and, if you are concerned or need help, go to your team.

Effective Team Communication

One of the care team leader's most important roles is to develop effective communication within the care team. Ask ahead of time who is comfortable with which tasks. One person cannot do everything, but everyone can do something. If you have a family member who wants to be of help and they do not live nearby, perhaps they can take on the role of research or finding services that could be of help. They may be able to help you financially since they are not able to help with daily chores, activities, and care.

Think creatively to fill the needs you currently have. Each person will have a team unique to them. As you connect with other caregivers you may find more team members whom you hadn't considered. Don't be afraid of trial and error. It is essential as a caregiver to give it your best shot and then check and adjust as you go. It is progress and not perfection that we seek.

Setting up regular meetings with clear communication helps to keep everyone on the same page. Times have changed and, in the post-pandemic world, we have increased our virtual presence significantly. Taking the time to get everyone up to speed is much easier in our digital age than it was when I began caregiving.

I used to keep information in notebooks, folders, and binders, but now records are easily stored or accessible on a cell phone in the palm of my hand. Also, a variety of caregiving apps are hitting the market, which allow for greater access and communication between team members. As our technological world continues to expand, it is likely that ever-increasing options will be available. Use these to your advantage to keep everyone informed and coordinated.

You may also find your care team needs specific training related to the care recipient's needs, such as learning about medical procedures and emergency needs or how to provide emotional support. Consider reaching out to an eldercare specialist or using the skills of a caregiver coach to support you. I have had the pleasure of working with families on this part of their journey and it can be an immense help as you navigate your new normal. If you are caring for a child with special needs, talk with your school staff, community resources, and medical teams to potentially cover training for your team.

We had a wonderful vision specialist, "Supreme Doreen," who worked with Isaac and provided much-needed information on blindness and the unique needs of those with vision loss to our family and education team members. Rely on these people to support you because, as I said earlier, "Everyone can do something, but one person cannot do everything."

Clear Expectations

Make sure you are setting clear expectations as the team leader regarding hopes for care and the boundaries and ground rules in place so you can avoid misunderstandings and minimize conflict. Caregiving can leave you with less in your tank, so the more information and expectations people understand from the beginning, the smoother the process will go.

With your team in place, having built connections and set boundaries, you can begin to put your care plan in place. This plan might be formal or informal and can include such items as schedules, specific tasks, medication management, and contingency plans. The more you can encourage your team and model collaboration, the more supportive your team will be and the better it will function.

Remember to regularly review your team members and their performance to sustain an effectively functioning group. You can adjust as often as you need to address the ever-changing needs of the care recipient and entire team. If you struggle or feel unprepared or overwhelmed by a leadership role, remember you can also assign this role to another if that makes sense for you. Practicing what you want to say and how you want to share information can be helpful if this is a new role for you.

Again, having a coach can be extremely helpful in this realm as well. They can support you in developing skill sets you may not have used or developed yet. In addition, in medically complex situations, you may want a healthcare case manager to help you cover your care team's medical needs. This can alleviate some added stress for you and distribute some of the responsibilities. You are limited only by your imagination in choosing your team and how it functions.

The Three A's

As you step into new roles and new expectations, I encourage you to think of what I call "The three A's", which are: acknowledge, accept, and ask.

ACKNOWLEDGE that you are a caregiver and begin to take the opportunity to process what that means to you in your life now and what it may mean as your journey continues to evolve. The American Journal of the Medical Sciences has referred to caregivers as "hidden patients" (Dr. V. Roche, 2009), who experience adverse effects on the emotional, social, financial, and spiritual aspects of their lives, collectively referred to as the "caregiver burden" (SH Zarit, PA Todd, and JM Zarit, first explained in a longitudinal study in *Gerontologist*, 1986).

Recognizing your role as a caregiver, in addition to the personal relationship you have with the person you care for, can be the first step toward better health outcomes for you. I like to think of this acknowledgement as a prescription; just as a pharmacist provides you with medication for your health, naming yourself as a caregiver can offer benefits for your mental, physical, and emotional well-being.

ACCEPT that you are going to be learning new things, things you may have never wanted to know. Also accept that you are only one person and cannot do everything alone. When someone offers help, allow them to support and encourage you. Building a strong, effective, and lasting team is crucial.

Finally, **ASK.** It can be difficult to ask for help, but it is necessary. Consider how you feel when someone allows you to help them; put yourself in that frame of mind when others want to help you. Let them help – they would not offer if they did not genuinely want to support you. Remember caregivers are also worthy and in need of the care they offer so selflessly to others.

We do not live or exist in a vacuum. We are designed for connection so do not let yourself become isolated or forget the strength that comes from being a member of a functioning team. Remember team simply means **T**ogether **E**veryone **A**chieves **M**ore. Embrace the kindness and compassion offered to you, recognizing that you are as worthy of care as those you tend to. Take it in, soak it up, and breathe deeply, affirming to yourself, "I am worthy of care."

You are enough.

By working together with others, you not only enhance the well-being of those you love but also nurture your own heart and spirit.

CHAPTER 3:
Chapter Questions and Workbook

Reflection Questions:

Do you have ideas on who might become part of your care team? Have you had the opportunity to connect with other caregivers? Have you acknowledged that you are a caregiver? Do you feel comfortable asking for and accepting help when it is offered? What are your thoughts on leading a care team? Do you believe you are worthy of care?

Journal Prompts:

- What strengths do you bring to caregiving and who might complement these strengths as you build a care team?

_____

_____

_____

_____

- If you could build your own dream team, what members would be a part of it and why?

_____

_____

_____

_____

_____

- Imagine a time in the future when you have your team set up. What does that look like and how has it affected your caregiving?

_____

_____

_____

_____

Action Steps:

Complete a table such as the one below to name your support systems and begin to develop your care team. You can also simply print the names of friends, family members, and professionals who could help. Consider their strengths and what they may contribute to the team.

Name	Relationship	Strengths/ Skills	Availability	Willingness	Potential Role
(name)	(e.g., friend)	(e.g., great listener)	(e.g., flexible)	(e.g., high)	(emotional support)

"It takes courage to demand time for yourself. At first glance, it may seem to be the ultimate in selfishness, a real slap in the face to those who love and depend on you. It's not. It means you care enough to want to see the best in yourself and give only the best in yourself to others." — Shane Paul

CHAPTER 4:
Caring for the Caregiver

When Isaac was airlifted to a larger hospital near us, my first prayer was that he would be alive when we arrived at the hospital an hour's drive away. When we overcame that hurdle and were trying to discover what had happened to cause the incident, the prayer became, "Please let him not have a progressive or life-ending illness." When that prayer was also answered, we just prayed that he would come home and that we would be able to manage. We realized how quickly life can change. In a matter of days, we had transformed from a family with two healthy children to a family in desperate need of care for one of those children.

After several days in the pediatric intensive care unit, life became a bit more settled and I found myself becoming accustomed to the routine of checking his chart, asking questions about his test results, status updates, and even finding time to smile or chat with nursing staff. The change from normal parenting routines of feeding, sleeping, and diaper-changing had gone out the window and a new reality had begun. I knew my typical developing child was now simply a faraway dream and I had entered a new world. This world was not one I had wished for or wanted but it was the one I had.

Quite honestly, after having already suffered through the death of my daughter the year before, there was a great deal of gratitude in these early days of the journey as Isaac had survived. I truly felt that any ability he gained beyond breathing was gravy. Each time he passed another medical test or a potential diagnosis was eliminated, it was cause for celebration. We did not know what had caused his illness and, it turns out, we would never know for certain. But he was here and that was all that mattered.

As he continued to stabilize and recover, it became clear that he would eventually return home. While this was certainly cause for rejoicing, it was also terrifying. In the hospital I felt secure knowing that medical personnel were always available. Any challenge or potential emergency would be met with an immediate response. How was this going to be possible when he was away from the medical setting? I was grateful for my educational background and courses in anatomy and neuroanatomy, although the information took on a whole new perspective as it related to my baby.

Before he could be released, we had to find two people to come to the hospital for training on the apnea monitoring system. Again, there was gratitude for neighbors and friends who came to the hospital to learn these skills. Without them we would have no backup for care. After several weeks, he was ready to come home, and the journey was about to become one that I had never even considered. It was overwhelming, terrifying, and a cause for celebration all at the same time.

> ***I was about to discover that the role of a caregiver is one that demands constant presence, both physically and emotionally.***

Becoming a Caregiver at Home

With each new day came a flurry of tasks and responsibilities that had to be carried out with patience, compassion, and unwavering commitment.

This new journey repeatedly tested my resilience, challenged my patience, and redefined the depths of my love for my child. As the new day started, the reality of my world hit me. It was just over three months since I had delivered Isaac, and I also had a four-year-old, Brenna, who needed her mom's time and attention.

I felt isolated, scared, and alone many of these early days. The weight of the responsibility felt crushing as the new normal set in. How I wished I would have felt more confident or capable at the time. The one thing I knew was, regardless of my fear and apprehension, I deeply loved my family and was committed to doing my absolute best to care for all of them, especially Isaac. All I could do was move forward into this world I had never envisioned for myself and become a tireless advocate for the needs of my son.

As I had taken a leave of absence from my job to care for Isaac, I was grateful Isaac's dad was able to keep working to support our family. He would help take over at the end of the day when I needed a break and was able to share the load around his work schedule.

The day-to-day routine became centered around caring for my daughter, specific care and medication schedules for Isaac, appointments, household chores, and meals to plan. There were now also therapies, visits from school staff, and activities to help Isaac grow and develop. I was happy to have contact with former coworkers in the Early Childhood Special Education Program, as it gave me a connection I desperately missed.

There was also homework which I took seriously – too seriously. I felt a weight descend upon me that would sit with me for years to come, the fear of not doing it right and not doing enough. I could only manage the fear by trying to control every outcome, which meant I was not truly allowing others to support me in the way I needed. It also caused a great deal of anxiety, which flowed into daily routines and seeped into all areas of my life. One thing became clear to me:

*When you release the things you hold so tightly,
it allows you to open your hand to receive.*

The Importance of Accepting Help and Making Self-Care a Lifestyle

One of the most important parts of day-to-day caregiving is being able to accept help. Accepting help as a caregiver is self-care. You may be starting to see a recurring theme in this book. I know and meet caregivers daily who struggle with self-care. I cannot stress enough the importance of building self-care into your daily life and routines to thrive as a caregiver.

*It is important to think of self-care not as a reward
but as a responsibility to yourself.*

I invested all my energy into caring for others and I see other caregivers doing the same. We care for others with diligence and commitment, yet we do not have the same sense of responsibility to ourselves. For that reason alone, let's address self-care first in our discussion of day-to-day caregiving.

Self-care may seem like a luxury when looking at all the tasks and activities that go along with caregiving. I believe it is time to change the concept of self-care into a necessity. Self-care is not something you get to do after all the things you have to do. If it were, it would never happen. Instead, self-care allows you to show up as your best self in the caregiving space. It does not have to be an activity; self-care is a lifestyle.

It is about being intentional in the smallest of spaces, and sometimes self-care can be as simple as pausing to take a deep breath. You will show up as your best self when you practice daily self-care, which will translate into better outcomes for the recipients of care.

There are several ways to use self-care to recharge. In fact, using the word "**RECHARGE**" is a handy way to remember to prioritize your self-care practices. These are useful for both caregivers and care recipients.

REST

R reminds us to find rest. It is the space of small breaks throughout the day to just pause, breathe deeply, and find a bit of peace. Breathing techniques such as box breathing, or square breathing are helpful to find restful pause. This technique is simple to practice, requires no equipment, and can be done anytime to decrease stress, clear your mind, and find focus. I used breathwork when completing range-of-motion exercises with Isaac. It allowed me to reset, and the calm was good for both of us.

If you are new to breathing techniques it can be helpful to sit in a chair or lie down with one hand on your chest and one on your stomach. If seated, remember to place your feet firmly on the floor to feel grounded. If you notice your chest rising but not your stomach, you are breathing in a shallow manner. Allow your belly to expand or rise in order to activate relaxation and breathe deeply. Also, if you are lying on your back, you will feel your back pressed against the floor or bed when you take deep breaths.

To practice box breathing, simply complete the following steps:
1. Breathe in while slowly counting to four. Feel the air enter and fill your lungs.
2. Hold your breath for four seconds and try not to inhale or exhale during this time.
3. Slowly exhale through your mouth for a count of four.
4. Pause and hold your breath again for a count of four.

Repeat this four-step process as many times as needed to fully relax.

Breathwork is one way to build rest into your day. Counting is a way to increase mindfulness and decrease the feeling of being overwhelmed that you often find in care situations. If a count of four is too long, start with a count of two and slowly build up your breath control.

Mindfulness and meditation are two other great options for finding space to rest while caring for others. Focus on the activities you do as you are doing them. Mindfulness can happen while washing dishes, cleaning your house, or completing care tasks. Simply staying in the moment is beneficial. I have heard other people describe it as staying where your feet are. In other words, be present. It is amazing the difference this makes!

EATING

E stands for eating. It is important to remember that our bodies need food for fuel. Eating the foods that fuel us and those we care for is important. Good nutrition can support the health of the care recipient and aid in their recovery and overall wellbeing. There were days when I would reach the end of the day and realize I had eaten nothing. Other days, I ate everything in sight.

Remember that food does not have a morality, and you aren't "good" or "bad" regardless of how you choose to nourish yourself. Quite honestly, sometimes coffee and a candy bar felt like just what I needed! You may have more energy and sustain your health and the health of your family by eating a rainbow of foods and trying to keep a balanced diet. In fact, with all the meal delivery service options which exist now, it can be easier to keep a balanced diet without having to meal plan along with all the other tasks you must do as a caregiver.

I also believe food prep parties with friends are a fantastic way to reduce isolation and have social connections if it is hard to leave the house. Pick several recipes, order in the supplies, and have friends join in for a meal prep extravaganza. You end up with connection, nutrition, and support in ways you may not have imagined. The care recipient may enjoy seeing old friends as well as it can seem familiar in a space that is frequently changing. Allowing friends to join you in caregiving duties is a win for your emotional well-being as well.

COMMUNICATION

C is for communication. As a caregiver, there is often a feeling of frustration if you are not getting the help you need. My question to you is, "Have you told someone?"

It is important to remember people don't necessarily know how you are feeling if you are not able to effectively communicate those feelings. Having regular check-in time with family, friends, secondary caregivers, and your support systems is crucial in daily caregiving.

I was an "I'm fine" or "I'm good" type of person much of the time, yet I was not always doing well. It took me a long time to be able to express my needs or to realize their value in the daily space of caregiving. Effective communication techniques, having a regular time to discuss and update your team, and setting boundaries are all helpful tools for the caregiver. Making sure your care recipient has the ability to communicate their journey is also essential. Do they have the ability to process their journey with you, with friends, or with a qualified professional? We all benefit from sharing our thoughts and feelings.

HEALTH

H stands for health. I am not referring only to the health of the care recipient at this point, but to your healthcare needs as a caregiver. Remember, if something happens to you, then the outcomes shift for everyone else. All too often, there are negative health outcomes for caregivers because they place all their needs on the back burner.

Monitoring your own health ranges from treating chronic conditions to setting up regular checkups. Both can keep your internal operating system functioning at the highest level possible. Do not forget to schedule your routine healthcare appointments and to see a doctor if you are unwell. Caregivers of all ages have reported a decline in their own health and well-being due to caregiving. You must prioritize your own health and well-being both physically and emotionally in order to continue to provide care for others.

ACCEPTING and ACKNOWLEDGING

A stands for accepting and acknowledging. You must accept you are doing the best you can with the situation as it exists. If you truly feel you could do better, be willing to look for ways to improve or ask for help from your loved ones or care team members. It can be easy to get stuck in a cycle of shame and guilt as a caregiver.

Acknowledging the very real and challenging space of caregiving is a way to honor your journey. Acknowledge that you are only one person and recognize that you are trying to support not only your life but the life and care of another. I don't think any of us who provide care enter this space with enough grace. It can become easy to beat ourselves up or to hold ourselves to a higher standard of care than we expect from others.

Connecting with others who understand the challenges of caregiving can be incredibly therapeutic. Support groups offer a safe space to share experiences, seek advice, and remind yourself that you are not alone in this journey.

Accepting and Acknowledging as the recipient of care may also be served by the opportunity to connect with others in the same or similar situations. When I was in outpatient rehabilitation, I was involved in a brain injury group with other professionals. This was both a support group and therapy. It helped me significantly to realize my feelings and experiences were shared by others. This decreased my feelings of loss and there was validation for what I was experiencing. Navigating a new way of life and the changes that had occurred was difficult and processing through it with professional help and with others experiencing the same journey was invaluable.

RESPITE

The second **R** in RECHARGE stands for respite. Respite care can provide you with much-needed breaks to reset and address your own needs without feeling guilty. This is an area in which your care team and secondary caregivers can help you. Respite does not have to be a monumental vacation or getaway. You could plan a short trip to a nearby town or park. Sometimes just a change of scenery is a wonderful way to renew yourself.

Take time to engage in a hobby or activity you enjoy. Get together with friends or family you don't see because of your caregiving responsibilities. Take a long drive with a friend or spend time alone in nature. You could book a hotel or Airbnb for a night or a weekend and get restorative sleep. The importance of respite and breaks in caregiving can help to prevent burnout, preserve relationships, and allow for a new perspective on your own identity outside of caregiving.

It is normal to feel like we don't deserve a break as caregivers. After all, the person we are caring for is the "important one". There is an excess amount of guilt and shame around the topic of leaving your care recipient with someone else. Relieving the guilt around taking breaks is essential for your physical and mental health as a caregiver. It is not unusual for caregivers to feel they must be constantly present to provide the care. This only leads to burnout and stress.

Taking time away is not a sign of weakness or neglect. In fact, it is a necessary step to sustain your own health in long-term care. By taking the opportunity to step away, you provide better care. This reset helps you to recover and return to care, providing you with an increased focus and ability to handle the demands of caregiving. and return to care providing with an increased focus and ability. You will be less likely to make mistakes or have accidents yourself.

Taking time off does not mean you are failing or inadequate in any way. In fact, the opposite is true. Your ability to care for yourself is a gift to the care recipient. I can tell you, from the perspective of a care recipient, that I wanted my team to get a break as well. You also feel guilty when you see your caregiver never getting a break. You don't want to be responsible for their descent and stress. Communication is key in this area as well so having the opportunity to talk about your needs whether you are a caregiver or care recipient is essential.

Building your support network and utilizing respite care options, whether that is family, friends, or professional services can improve your overall experience as a caregiver. Breaks give you the opportunity to prevent the emotional fatigue and feelings of resentment or exhaustion that may surface when you don't allow yourself to practice self-care. Relieving guilt starts by acknowledging that caregiving is not a one-person show. It is a shared responsibility and recognizing that is the beginning of practicing self-compassion which is an integral part of the journey.

One of the most challenging aspects of caregiving is overcoming the feelings of guilt that arise when taking time for yourself—whether it's a short break, a getaway, or simply a moment to relax. Many caregivers struggle with the belief that any time spent away from their duties is somehow 'neglecting' their responsibilities. Intellectually, we all know the importance of self-care, but emotionally, it can be incredibly difficult to put into practice. That's why this chapter is so vital—it reminds us that taking care of ourselves is not a luxury, but a necessity for providing the best care possible to our loved ones.

GET ENOUGH SLEEP

G is for getting enough sleep. Sleep is often underrated when you are a caregiver. Isaac did not sleep through the night until he was at least

12 years old and then it was inconsistent. We underestimate the role sleep deprivation plays in the caregiving world. Sleep is the time when our bodies regenerate and repair. When you don't get adequate sleep there can be significant implications including a weakened immune system, higher risk of chronic conditions, anxiety, depression, and safety concerns. You are more likely to make mistakes related to care, be at greater risk of accidents, and increase already challenging stress levels. Caregivers and care recipients are both in need of restorative sleep.

Ensuring healthy sleep patterns is necessary not only for their well-being but also for the quality of care they provide. Hiring overnight staff or asking friends to cover a few nights so you can sleep could be another possibility.

EXERCISE

Finally, the last **E** is for exercise. It is not necessary to approach exercise as an all-or-nothing activity. Doing a few basic movements or exercises during the day is already helpful. Setting a timer throughout your day to remind yourself can be one way to get exercise into your daily routine. Movement can be built into the care plan for your care recipient too. It is important to work your body the way your body works. Relying on physical and occupational therapists or a personal trainer who specializes in post-rehab treatment can also be helpful if your care recipient is in the rehabilitation process.

Since my accident and because of medical restrictions, I take a break every 45 to 60 minutes during my day to change positions, stretch, move my body, or complete a few repetitions of a specific exercise. By the end of the day, those three to five repetitions during each break have added up. Also, if their condition allows it, you can get your care recipient involved too. This can provide both of you with activity which improves physical and mental health, boosts energy levels, improves cognitive function, increases circulation, and decreases your overall stress.

Establish Routines to Improve Time Management and Reduce Stress

In addition to caring for yourself as a caregiver, there are many ways to structure the daily tasks and routines of the care recipient. Consistent routines from waking up to bedtime as well as for meals and general care can make a dramatic difference. When you have a set routine, it is easier to avoid forgetting tasks that need to be completed. It is also helpful to take the time and opportunity to look at all the tasks which need to be completed and to prioritize them. In our ever-evolving, technology-driven world there are endless ways to track and set up routines.

Whether it is as simple as a pen and paper list, a shared spreadsheet, or an app as a digital assistant, the choice is yours. There is no shortage of options; you just need to discover how you work best and what fits your specific situation. The consistency and predictability of routines can be useful in reducing anxiety and confusion for care recipients. It also allows the caregiver the ability to manage their time and responsibilities more effectively.

Knowing what needs to be completed and when makes it easier when secondary caregivers handle the routine as well. I used a large, magnetic dry erase board which showed the tasks which needed completion every day. When hired caregivers were present, they would place a magnet in the grid once they completed a task. Having this visual system in place allowed me to see what tasks still needed attention. I felt more secure knowing whether there were activities that were my responsibility, and in this way, I was able to make sure all of Isaac's needs were being met. I would feel less stressed if I knew what had happened in my absence. This was also helpful if I was not there when hired caregivers left for the day.

The ability to look at the needs of the care recipient and to prioritize physical, emotional, and cognitive needs can be helpful in planning a daily schedule. If you know his or her emotional state tends to change at midday you may choose activities to support it, such as a period of social connection or relaxation. Physical activities and therapies may be best scheduled in the morning when they are more alert and awake. The bottom line is to evaluate your routines and schedules to see what best serves you and those you care for.

Not every task needs to be accomplished by the primary caregiver. Work toward becoming comfortable delegating tasks and routines. Remember, once you delegate, you have passed the torch. I absolutely struggled with this. If you want to have help moving forward, try not to micromanage or take back a task you have delegated. It can be hard on relationships, and it simply keeps you stuck in the space of doing everything. This is a clear path to burnout and resentment. Just because something does not happen exactly the way you do it does not make it wrong. Done is better than perfect in most situations and you build connections with others when you share responsibility.

Maintain Balanced and Consistent Flow

After my accident I struggled, as I was not able to provide the care I always had for Isaac. I was used to balancing so many things and felt quite accomplished after 20 years of caregiving. I wanted to function at the same level, but it simply was not possible with my brain injury and other medical issues. My doctor, the same one who admitted me to inpatient rehabilitation, once told me to strive for 80 percent for 80 percent of the time. I continue to strive for this balance in my life and I can honestly say that advice is among the most helpful I received on my recovery journey.

Having a balanced and consistent flow of daily tasks can lend a sense of calm and ease to days that are often difficult for any number of reasons. Caregiving is fraught with unexpected and unplanned occurrences. If you have a regular schedule, it can help when those unexpected changes occur. Prioritizing the most critical issues can be helpful if something happens to you as a caregiver. This way, if another caregiver is stepping in, there is an idea of which tasks are the most crucial and which can be set aside for a while.

If possible, continue to include the person needing care in the discussions related to schedules and priorities. You may find you both have quite different ideas about the items at the top of the list. Communication is key whether you are speaking to a care team member, the care recipient, or a substitute caregiver. Taking the time to regularly evaluate the routines and making necessary adjustments can also improve outcomes and make the days flow more smoothly.

Create Backup Plans and Time Buffers

Another important part of the day-to-day routine is to have backup plans in place. This is another area in which your care team can be of help. Do you know who can step in if you are ill or need to be away from home? Who are your go-to team members? It is helpful to have more than one person who can fill in if something happens to you. Make sure you have these conversations early and often in the caregiving journey. We never know when something can change, and it is far less stressful if you have a plan in place.

Adding in buffer time is something I learned in my recovery. Know the time it takes to complete most daily tasks and travel. I had a great deal of difficulty with processing time and the passage of time after my accident so, if I needed to be somewhere, I learned to plan for the time it took and then I would add another 15 to 30 minutes as a buffer. This helped decrease my anxiety and when I had to drive, which was traumatic, I had an extra cushion, so I did not feel the added burden of thinking I was going to be late. This is a helpful idea for caregivers as it relates to daily routines because we never know what unplanned or unexpected task is going to be needed. The decrease in stress I experienced by adding in buffer time made me wish I had done it years earlier.

Schedules and routines are only as useful as you make them. If you find yourself lacking flexibility because you are so stuck and tied to routine, you may miss opportunities for spontaneity and fun in your caregiving. It's easy to fall into the trap of overscheduling, especially with the endless tasks that come up each day. While it might feel necessary to fill every moment with activity, being constantly overscheduled can actually harm your well-being. When you don't leave room for rest or reflection, you risk burnout, increased stress, and a decrease in the quality of your relationships. Balance is key – creating space in our schedules for downtime is just as important as tackling our to-do lists.

Look for ways to find time for fun, relaxation, and self-care even if it is just a few minutes throughout your day. Remind yourself that it is OK to step away from activities that have little to no return for you and your care recipient. Caregiving can be isolating, so let yourself enjoy those moments when you can let go and relax. This flows back into your life and affects all those who surround you.

Create Flexible Plans that Work for Your Caregiving Journey

By starting small and gradually building a daily routine which works for you, there will be opportunities for acceptance and adjustment along the journey you have embarked upon. Remember to keep your own routine of self-care and the activities you need for your life as well. Implementing daily care routines is an important part of the caregiving experience, offering stability and comfort for the care recipient while helping caregivers manage their responsibilities and stay organized.

Recognizing the benefits and challenges of routines allows caregivers to create flexible plans that meet the unique needs of their loved ones. With contemplative planning, clear and effective communication, and regular adjustments, routines can improve the quality of life for everyone. By setting up and embracing routines that fit their unique needs, caregivers can create better care patterns while also prioritizing their own well-being. This will make the caregiving journey a more manageable and rewarding experience.

Taking the time to work together with all those involved can create a sense of community that may often be lacking in the caregiving space. We all want caregivers and care recipients to have the best possible outcomes and opportunities to thrive. With careful consideration and diligence, a consistent schedule and routines can be a step in the right direction.

CHAPTER 4:
Chapter Questions and Workbook

Reflection Questions:

What do you think of when you hear about self-care? How do you currently spend your time? Where can you find space to care for yourself? What strategies have you tried to care for yourself and how successful were they?

Journal Prompts:

- Write about a time when you nurtured yourself. What did you do and how did you feel when you were the priority?

_____

_____

_____

_____

- How can you prioritize self-care in a way that feels possible and sustainable for you now?

_____

_____

_____

STILL, I RISE

_____

_____

Action Steps:

Watch a Video:
Melody Shares How to Recharge:

http://www.melodyvachal.com/how-to-recharge

Using the wellness wheel, place a dot on the concentric circles within each section to indicate your current wellness level. Refer to the RECHARGE strategies in this chapter, marking closer to the center if an area needs improvement and farther out if you're thriving. This will give you a visual snapshot of where you're doing well and where you may want to focus more attention.

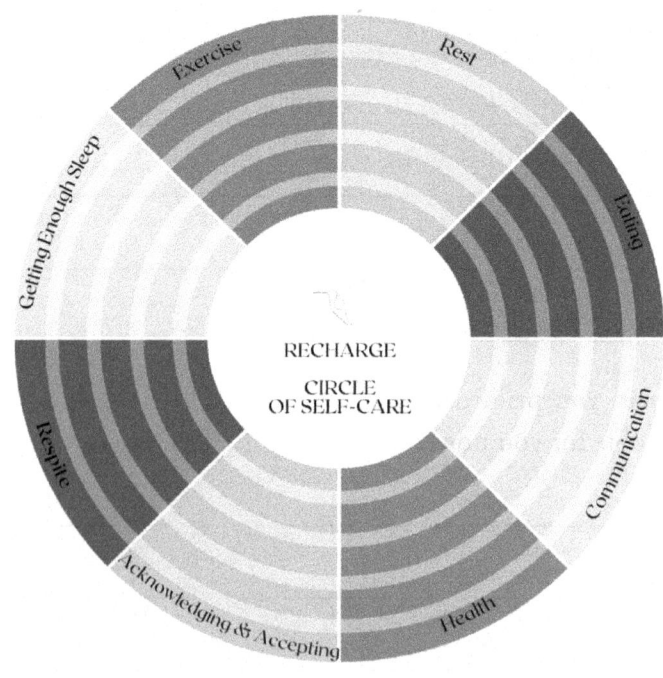

"A hero is an ordinary individual who finds the strength to persevere and endure in spite of overwhelming obstacles." — Christopher Reeve

CHAPTER 5:
Emotional and Psychological Impact of Caregiving

When I was a child, I was quite a talker. I was the youngest of six in a rural North Dakota farm family and had my own voice. My siblings would agree with that! My mother would try to find peace in the home by offering me a quarter to stop talking for five minutes. I don't remember ever making much money from this enticing offer.

My father was a storyteller who could enthrall you with the details of his childhood and family history. One story he often shared was of me as a young child of 5 or 6. At the time, my dad was driving a bulk truck delivering fuel to local farmers and filling the tanks on their farms. Sometimes he would come by our home and pick me up for a delivery so he could have company on his route. I believe my mother may have suggested it so she could have a bit of silence. He told how, as we drove, I chattered on and kept him engaged and entertained. One day, I was chatting away when suddenly there was silence. When he looked over, I had fallen asleep! So, he drove on, and a brief time later, when I woke up, I began speaking exactly where I had left off in the conversation and hadn't missed a beat. Is it surprising that I became a speech-language pathologist who had the privilege of helping others develop their communication skills for over 30 years? I think not.

Along this communication-filled journey my mother took the opportunity to remind me, "If you can't say something nice, don't say anything at all." It seems like reasonable advice to a child dealing with friends and developing social skills. It is important to think of others and how the words we say might affect them. I did not realize how deeply I took that to heart. I began to store up those unspoken thoughts and words. Sometimes I would think about the unkind words I might say but eventually, I got used to pushing them down along with the feelings that went with them. This seems to be where my emotional processing of those feelings got stuck.

Learning to Express Needs, Thoughts, and Emotions

By nature, I am a positive person, which has served me well in both my recovery and in caregiving. The challenge with this is not feeling a full spectrum of emotions. After my accident, I was diagnosed with PTSD (post-traumatic stress disorder), and while collaborating with a therapist, we talked about where in my body I felt sadness or anger. I really had no answer or ability to process many feelings besides fear. It took me a long time to realize I could express a variety of emotions.

Before that, I could not fully express my needs and thoughts related to feelings. I just stuffed down my feelings, kept moving, and kept a smile on my face. It took me a long time to recognize that I had a voice and valid feelings. I needed to learn to express them to be at my best emotionally and to prioritize my mental health.

The impact of mental and emotional health in the caregiving journey is something which cannot be underrated. As caregivers, we are often silenced by the needs of others to the point where we become lost in the process. It seems almost selfish to consider our feelings when the person we care for is struggling and trying to adjust to their new normal. There does not seem to be a time or place for the caregiver to address the emotional toll caregiving has placed upon them.

Adding to this is the high frequency of becoming a caregiver without any warning or preparation, which leaves many of us in a state that includes countless unprocessed emotions. So many caregivers are struggling to hold on and are plagued by guilt, shame, grief, loss, and the list goes on and on. They also fully hold those they care for in a space of love and compassion. This is part of why emotional well-being becomes so complicated in the caregiving space. We feel conflicted as caregivers, and it is difficult to express the hard emotions we are feeling.

Recognizing the Mental Health Needs of Care Recipients

We must also remember to focus on and address the needs of the individual receiving care in this equation. When I was lying in a hospital bed unable to turn over or feed myself, I was distraught and dealing with a great deal of emotional pain. This was present along with all my physical issues. Looking back now I realize that no mental health practitioner was a part of my early journey. I could not process many of these feelings for years after the accident.

As a society and as those who support people receiving care, we must become more aware of mental health needs in the care continuum. This is true not only for individuals but also for society as a whole. Remember that care recipients also experience fear, anger, depression, and gratitude. The emotional toll of watching others care for you is very real as well. I was afraid for my family. I worried the challenges of my care and recovery would break them.

I felt guilty over having to receive care and adding more stress to a home life which was already difficult. It was heartbreaking to realize that I had always felt like a part of the solution and now I felt like a huge part of a problem. I wanted nothing more than to be able to turn back the hands of time, but that only happens in the movies. So, I needed to move forward to heal my mind as well as my body.

As I healed, I felt like I needed to heal physically and emotionally, and I also believed I had to have even more achievements so I could prove my worthiness and be better than I was before. To show I was capable, I became certified as a personal trainer, earned a master's certification as a health and wellness coach, and even ran three half marathons, despite never being a runner! In the midst of my healing, I pushed myself to these accomplishments, seeking to rise stronger than ever before. While I am proud of these achievements, it is useful to realize I was enough and valuable just as I was and trying to prove my value through external means was something I needed to address.

I was lucky to be able to use mental health therapy later in the healing process, but for many people, there are significant disparities evident in accessing these services. This is a significant issue which needs serious consideration so that everyone in our communities can receive the help they so desperately need in challenging times.

Developing a Positive Mindset

Building resilience as you receive care is vital for mental and emotional well-being. It enhances quality of life, adaptation to loss, and can contribute to developing a positive outlook regardless of the challenges associated with receiving care. It is important for everyone in the care space to work toward developing a positive mindset and to take the time to celebrate a person's strengths and achievements even if they look vastly different than they have in the past. This sense of self-worth and competence is important to improving mental health outcomes. Everyone wants to feel their value and being on the receiving end of care is often a space of feeling "less than."

Working toward gratitude and developing a gratitude practice was something I found incredibly helpful following my accident. Focusing on small things I was grateful for made me look for more aspects of life that held positive emotions. The practice of gratitude awareness increases the release of the neurotransmitters dopamine and serotonin which uplift your mood and create feelings of well-being and pleasure. Gratitude can also improve cognitive function and emotional resilience. It also lowers stress and anxiety and can increase connections in the brain, which was significant for me as an individual with a brain injury. The more you can express and feel gratitude, the more grateful you become, which makes life a little bit brighter and lightens the emotional load.

Setting and achieving small goals is important for both care recipients and caregivers in terms of mental health. Feeling a sense of purpose in daily events and having the ability to carry out a goal keeps you looking forward. Being able to see possibilities in the future, even if they look quite different than you expected, can brighten the outlook on a challenging journey.

Breaking goals down into small steps can lessen feelings of being overwhelmed in the difficult phase of recovery and allows you to see growth even in the space of long-term disability. I used goal setting with my physical and mental health therapy, and it allowed me to feel a sense of control in situations that had felt out of control from the start.

The importance of mental health also becomes significant as we look at the long-term effects of caregiving. We already know caregivers are at risk for physical health challenges, including the development of chronic illnesses such as heart disease and high blood pressure due to stress and the demands of caregiving. We addressed the importance of prioritizing your own health as a caregiver in Chapter 4 as it relates to self-care. The physical health needs are often more obvious and noted by providers, although as caregivers we often ignore them.

Mental health concerns are not addressed enough, and we continue to feel some level of stigma about sharing those struggles. Talking about our own mental health, sharing our stories, and continuing to treat mental health as a part of overall health is necessary for society, especially those in the caregiving space.

Experiencing Grief and Loss

Grief and loss are significant as we cycle through times of remembering what was and mourning what will never be again. They cannot be minimized, and these emotions can come up repeatedly. They also look different depending on who you care for. As the caregiver of a child with special needs, I would experience grief at the milestones Isaac did not meet or at the times he should have been making them. When my youngest son's development leapfrogged over Isaac's I mourned, even while rejoicing in what both Shane and Isaac were accomplishing.

Even now, watching my grandson – a toddler – play with toys like those Isaac enjoys as an adult, brings me a bit of grief and sadness. It does not last as long as it used to and it isn't as deep, but the sadness is still there. The loss of what I thought would happen is also accompanied by gratitude for all Isaac has achieved. It is not an either-or situation but a "both-and."

When I was caring for my dad, I grieved the changes in his health conditions and the continued and repeated hospitalizations. I grieved for him as he mourned the loss of my mother and navigated a new world without her. The point is, we need to be better at sharing these experiences so we can normalize our emotional health. If we do not process grief and acknowledge its place in our lives, it takes a toll on our emotional well-being and mental health. Remember, grief may last a lifetime, and it looks different from day to day. Give yourself the grace to hold the grief and feel no shame in releasing it. There is no right way to grieve and allowing yourself the space to do so is a step toward emotional well-being.

Managing Guilt and Shame

Guilt and shame are emotions which come up repeatedly in a caregiving journey. How can we feel overwhelmed, tired, and adrift in an endless sea of emotions when our loved ones are "truly suffering"? We feel guilty because we still have our health or the ability to be independent in our lives when our loved one may not. Guilt also surfaces if we think about taking time away from caregiving responsibilities. We may believe we no longer have the right to enjoy ourselves or have experiences our loved one can no longer take part in.

Shame rears its head when we believe we are not doing a respectable job of caring for someone else. We feel defective if something goes wrong, we make a mistake, or if our loved ones are not thriving in our care. These feelings often turn into an inner dialogue which challenges our overall worth as a person. Guilt and shame often surface when we begin to have resentment about being a caregiver and the great impact it has on our lives.

As a parent of a child with special needs, I felt guilty if I were jealous over activities my friends or other families were able to experience. Our life was not less than, it was different, but it did not always feel that way. As I watched other families, I mourned what would never happen. I expected to care for a child but did not predict this care would continue for the rest of my life. It was partly the loss of the dream of what I believed life would be. It can be helpful to try and release expectations as they often resurface as resentments which serve no good purpose for our mental and emotional wellness.

Also remember not to let someone else's happenings affect your happiness. This can be related to comparing ourselves to others or to the drama that can be present in our lives and the lives of others. Getting pulled into other people's emotions and challenges is a struggle which can significantly affect our emotional wellness. It is easy to get stuck in the space of "compare and despair" in a caregiving space. In a world shaped by social media, we can quickly find ourselves comparing our insides to another's outsides. Everyone has challenges and parts of life which are more complicated than others. When you only see the highs, it can be hard not to feel resentment.

Persistent guilt can also contribute to increased stress and burnout as you try to achieve more or push yourself beyond your limits. Guilt can cloud your judgment to the point that you are not making the best decisions related to your needs and those of the care recipient.

One strategy for managing guilt is the practice of self-compassion. Acknowledging an awareness of guilt as a normal part of the journey and realizing we all struggle can help us frame our journey in the context of the larger society. Attempting to minimize expectations or set realistic expectations about the scope of your abilities as a caregiver and accepting that you are only one person can also be helpful. No one is perfect, and it is important to prioritize progress over perfection in your caregiving and in life.

The Importance of Relationships

Finally, seeking support from trusted friends, family, or support groups can also be of great benefit to the caregiver. Realizing that you may have to search for a support system or group which is supportive versus stagnant is crucial. At times you may find people stuck and unable to move forward, so figure out if that support serves you or needs to be let go. Maybe it is not the right group or even the right time. If something does not work out in the present, it may be useful at another point in your life.

Anger and frustration over the balance of responsibilities can be an aspect of the emotional toll of caregiving. If you are unable to communicate well with a care partner or family member over sharing the load, it is easy to become stuck in a negative frame of mind. Taking the time to plan and have frequent conversations about day-to-day and long-term caregiving can help to alleviate irritation and bitterness. It can be helpful to have a third party – a friend, therapist, or coach – work with you as you focus on communication to diffuse the anger and frustration.

Remember, it is common to have these feelings, and it is best to work through them, so your relationships do not suffer as a result. Statistics on divorce are already high and adding in a child with special needs or chronic illness sends them even higher. Even if the outcome is divorce, taking the time to improve your communication skills and co-parenting strategies only improves the outcomes for your children, no matter what age they are. This can improve the overall mental health of the family and lead to further healing and better health outcomes generally. Additionally, if you and a former spouse are parents, you will be in each other's lives in some way, shape, or form in the future, so learning to coexist will improve engagement and boost happiness for everyone involved.

Much of what changes as a caregiver occurs in the realm of your social connections, and you can feel isolated physically and emotionally. You may lose friendships as you do not have the same availability to keep in touch with friends. They may not understand your new normal or feel they do not want to bother you when you already have so many irons in the fire. Loneliness is a reality for caregivers. Online caregiving groups and forums can be a way to develop an understanding of your journey and may be a fantastic way to set up new connections. Shared common experiences often create a bond which can be an important way to alleviate the mental health challenges of caregiving.

Maintaining contact with family and friends through calls, video chats, or in-person visits is an essential part of prioritizing your emotional wellness. Pursuing hobbies and interests by yourself or with friends can bring you a sense of normalcy and keep you in contact with others who are important to you. Having even one or two friends with whom you can check in on a regular basis and share your true self is invaluable for your mental and emotional well-being.

Identifying as a Caregiver

When we look at the variety of feelings, emotions, and caregiver challenges it becomes clear why improving mental health outcomes for caregivers and care recipients is so vital. One of the key first steps in the journey is simply being able to identify as a caregiver. Establishing the critical role we play, in addition to the relationship we share with our care recipient, allows us to not only confirm our experience, but also to bring awareness of the effort and emotional investment involved in our journey. This can reduce our feelings of isolation and frustrations involved in caregiving. When you recognize and claim the title of caregiver it can be an added access point for accepting the help necessary to thrive emotionally.

When you add the layer of caregiver to the relationships you hold with those you care for, it can help you realize that you have dual roles and responsibilities. It took me a long time to understand I was more than a mother, daughter, wife, or friend. I was and am a caregiver. The depths of that word and all its connotations help us appreciate the need for added support in mental and emotional health.

Understanding all that accompanies caregiving can be an encouragement for caregivers to seek mental health support or therapy to manage all the complicated feelings and emotions which are part of caring for one another.

By identifying as a caregiver, you also open the door to more resources, services, and supports which can simplify the experience. There may be training programs, workshops, and information which can support your mental health if you begin to understand the layers that go with caregiving. It can also help you to develop a sense of community with others who wear the caregiver label. Shared understanding can help you reduce the isolation you may experience. Also, caregivers who recognize and share their role can be a beacon of hope for others who are new to or struggling with their journey in a new and uncharted space.

When you identify as a caregiver, you can advocate for yourself and caregivers in your community and society in general. Understanding this role can encourage the prioritization of personal health and well-being and lend credibility to the experience of caregiving. It promotes a sense of balance when you begin to realize that you are more than just a family member doing what anyone does for someone they love or a friend who cares and wants to help. Your ability to care for another improves by accessing added training and resources to improve your mental health, and it may lead to better decision-making about care.

There may also be more legal and financial aid available to you as a caregiver, which can significantly decrease stress and help to manage the economic impact of caregiving. Finally, acknowledging your role as a caregiver can help you recognize the value you add and the contribution you are making not only to your loved one but as an advocate for the needs of caregivers within the community and beyond.

Claiming the title of caregiver can often improve mental health simply by advocating for your own needs such as support, your rights as a caregiver, and societal policy changes which can improve the lives of caregivers in years to come at the local, state, and national levels. Our systems and our society need to hear about the roles caregivers play so we can address the public health and economic challenges that are occurring for caregivers across our nation every day.

Caregiver mental health has significant impacts on individuals, families, employers, and society. Family caregivers, mostly women, are providing billions of dollars in unpaid care, often in addition to holding paid employment. The stresses of trying to work and care for a loved one are exhausting and we must do better at supporting caregivers in this often-invisible role they encompass. For family caregivers to continue to bear the burden of care we must increase our understanding of the caregivers in our society. Their mental health needs must be addressed for them to sustain the roles of caregiving. If we neglect prioritizing mental health support for caregivers, our society will suffer.

The Impact of Mental Health on Caregiving

We know the mental health of caregivers has a direct impact on the care they can provide. If we neglect to acknowledge the stress, anxiety, and depression that often goes with those in caregiving spaces, the individuals receiving care may be affected as well. Without mental health support, these caregivers may suffer in silence and struggle to keep the commitment, patience, empathy, and level of care needed to sustain effective caregiving.

This lessened level of care changes the quality of life of the care recipients and can lead to increased hospitalizations and overall poorer health consequences. Supportive systems which improve mental health outcomes establish better-prepared and more supportive caregivers. These caregivers in turn can provide a higher standard of care, are better equipped for long-term caregiving, and can model better health and well-being for those they support and others who view their journey.

The economic impact of caregiver mental health is also significant. Stressed and overwhelmed workers have higher rates of absenteeism, reduced workloads, and added financial strain in their families. Employers may experience decreased productivity and more healthcare costs as both caregivers and care recipients may need medical support. When caregivers are unable to cope with the challenges of caregiving, professional care needs to be increased, which adds to the economic impact of public health and increased reliance on government spending.

When caregivers feel they must give up significant aspects of their personal life to care for another, they lose social connections and engagement. Not only does this isolation worsen their mental health and overall quality of life, but it forces them to forego activities they used to enjoy. Communities see changes as their caregiver members withdraw from community involvement and volunteerism due to the significant mental health challenges of caregiving.

This impact is noted not only by the current caregiver but the generations that follow. Children of caregivers may be viewing the struggles their loved ones have encountered, leading to their own mental health issues and concerns. Our population continues to age, and the silver tsunami is upon us. The "silver tsunami" is a term used to describe the rapid aging of the global population, particularly the large wave of baby boomers reaching retirement age. As this demographic ages, there is an expected increase in the number of older adults who will need healthcare, long-term care, and other support services. The demand for caregiving will only increase, and caregiver mental health will continue to be an urgent issue. Without the support needed to address mental health in caregiving we continue to face a crisis in the ability to find qualified caregivers.

We must strive to find better and easier access to mental health services, help caregivers access the respite and breaks they need for their own wellness, and encourage workplaces to develop policies and programs to support family caregivers. By speaking out and reducing the stigma that often goes with mental health issues, we can encourage not only care for the caregivers but also for the communities. Supporting caregivers through improved mental health allows communities and society to build a more sustainable future for the caregivers of today and tomorrow.

CHAPTER 5:
Chapter Questions and Workbook

Reflection Questions:

What are your current emotions related to caregiving? Do you have someone to talk to about your feelings? Who do you rely on for emotional support?

What experiences, if any, do you have with accessing support for your mental and emotional health? Was this helpful for you?

What are your feelings related to grief and loss?

Journal Prompts:

Think about a recent situation that was emotionally challenging.

- What happened?

_____

_____

_____

_____

_____

- How did you feel?

_____

_____

- How did you react?

- What did you learn and what might you do differently next time?

Write about a time when you felt supported, or you handled an emotional challenge well. What was the experience and what can you learn from it or apply to your current situation?

_____

_____

_____

Action Steps:

Research online support groups for caregivers. Find out their meeting times, locations, and what they focus on. Take the opportunity to attend a meeting and discover whether it is helpful for you.

Take an emotional inventory of the feelings you are experiencing. Look at the emotion, name the trigger and your response, and see if you can devise an alternative response. You can journal these or use the table below as an example.

Emotion	Trigger/Situation	Response	Alternative
Sadness	Loved one no longer remembers you	Tears, isolating or withdrawing	Call a friend or family member to talk

"Our lives begin to end the day we become silent about the things that matter." — Martin Luther King

CHAPTER 6:
Advocacy and Communication

Have you ever been in a situation where you were so angry and overwhelmed you were ready to blow a gasket? When every time you tried to express your feelings, all you could do was rant? Trying to advocate for the needs of your loved one can seem like an uphill battle with no one listening. So how do you grow in your ability to manage tricky situations with clarity and assertiveness instead of seething with anger and aggression? You may have heard you can catch more flies with honey than vinegar. The same idea applies as we discuss advocacy and effective communication.

Advocacy in caregiving refers to the active role caregivers play in ensuring the care recipient's needs, preferences, and rights are respected and met. It involves speaking up on behalf of the care recipient, particularly when they may be unable to do so themselves due to illness, disability, or cognitive decline. Caregiver advocacy encompasses many areas, including medical decisions, access to services, legal rights, and ensuring the dignity and well-being of the care recipient are maintained.

At the core, advocacy is about representing the best interests of the person being cared for and navigating complex systems such as healthcare, education, insurance, and social services and accessing necessary resources. When considering advocacy and communication, it is important to support a level of cooperative team building. Our chapter on building a care team covered information on being the coach of your care team. Our work in advocacy often parallels the need to effectively and efficiently express your needs with assertiveness and clear communication. That is not to say you are only able to express positive thoughts and emotions. There are times when the exact opposite is true and challenging situations must be rectified.

You may meet team members and providers who have areas of expertise, and it is wise to avail yourself of their talents and knowledge. This is a wonderful opportunity to expand your resources and gain added awareness of specific issues related to your care situation. However, I believe as you work with your care team and providers, it is important to remember that, and it is wise to avail yourself of their talents and knowledge.

It is important to develop the ability to advocate and develop the skills necessary to build trust and rapport, find providers who are actively engaged, and manage the emotional situation of caregiving with effective communication techniques. Being part of a team is essential, as is communicating your needs in a manner that builds rapport and trust with those who are there to support you and the ones you care for.

When you prepare the soil before planting the seeds of advocacy, you will have much better results. Hard ground and bad seeds lead to less-than-desirable outcomes. Never doubt your knowledge, experience, or understanding of your own life. The journey of caregiving is full of twists and turns, and you will find it necessary to make challenging decisions. You will be expected to figure out the best options for everything from care partners to treatment options to educational programming. In these realms, it will be necessary to manage things you never even imagined. You will be dealing with any number of systems and – as is often the case in large organizations – it may seem the right hand does not know what the left is doing.

We have all been in situations in which the answer you get to a question varies from person to person and day to day. This can cause a great deal of frustration and annoyance. For someone who already has a very full plate, it can seem unfair that we also have to take on systems that can be overwhelming. How do you even start and in which direction do you head first? This is the space where effective communication and advocacy come into play.

Self-advocacy as the recipient of care is an important space to occupy. As a care recipient you are entitled to specific rights. Taking the time to understand your rights will help you in knowing whether those rights are being violated. If you can take part in your care planning and engage with your caregiver to access support networks, use available resources, and develop self-advocacy skills, do so. The more engaged you are, the better you can advocate for yourself.

Unfortunately, there are times when care recipients are at an elevated risk of neglect, exploitation, or abuse. Being able to share your experiences as a recipient of care is critical. If you are not getting the care you need, find out what options you have. If a provider is not a good fit for you let someone know or make a change. Research alternatives if you are unsatisfied with your current care or ask for help.

If that is not an easy undertaking for you, allowing your caregiver to support you through their efforts can be a way for your voice to be heard. As you work together to form a cohesive team you can develop better people skills, discover unknown strategies and strengths, strengthen your relationship with your caregiver, and hopefully have an important impact on your care.

The Power of Advocacy

The benefits of advocacy are even greater than one might imagine. Positive outcomes go with the space of advocacy. An increased sense of confidence comes with the development of advocacy skills. Knowing you are there to support the best outcomes in both mental and physical health is empowering to care partners and develops skills and strengths you may not have even known you had. You may strengthen the bond between you and those you care about when you spend time advocating for their specific needs.

Often the tables are turned in caregiving and we are advocating for someone who used to care for us. Maybe it is a parent, grandparent, or even a dear friend. Being able to use your skills and talents to support them is truly a gift and a recognition of the special bond you share. The times spent with my father when we were at medical appointments or in care situations created extra time together, and I cared for him in ways that tapped my skills and told him how important he was to me. I will never regret the opportunities I had to ensure he had the best possible care. He was always so grateful for my time and energy, and it was a gift I could give that was unique to me.

Taking the time and energy to support a loved one allows you the opportunity to express patience and empathy. You are also helping them navigate systems that may be too much for them to do on their own. When advocating as a caregiver you will find a sense of power in communicating your truth. So often we enter this caregiving world with no warning and no voice. Using your voice and your knowledge to support your loved one not only improves their life but it helps you take back your power.

Acting in the role of advocacy provides a stronger likelihood of achieving improved health outcomes. Approaching each interaction with an understanding of your specific needs, the significance of the overall problem, and the needs of the person receiving care allows you to become a supportive and engaged partner. This level of support is clear to providers and can be one of the first steps in building a strong working relationship where your advocacy is seen as a strength.

Developing Advocacy and Communication Skills

Developing skills for advocacy is not a walk in the park. There are also challenges to advocacy. When you are already in the space of day-to-day caregiving, time and energy are precious commodities. There do not seem to be enough hours in the day to do all the things that must be done. It may seem too overwhelming and not worth the tradeoff when you are exhausted with a full plate. Finding the time and space to learn about policies, procedures, and systems is difficult when you are dealing with limited bandwidth.

It can be emotionally draining to continue digging for answers to challenging questions and searching when it seems you have exhausted all the possibilities. The constant search for resources, support, and treatments must be balanced with the daily care you provide. There can be a financial strain that affects overall stress levels in this endeavor. Pairing that with feeling unprepared to be an advocate due to lack of assertiveness, difficulty with communication skills, or simply not knowing where to start can add stress to an already stressful life.

The strength of advocacy lies in consistent practice over time. You don't have to figure it out all at once and for those of us in the space of long-term caregiving, it can be a development of skills over time. In all new situations there is a learning curve that must be addressed, and advocacy and effective communication are more steps in the process.

One of the most important first steps in advocating is building relationships formed on trust and rapport. Having a provider who listens to your concerns and encourages you to engage with them in partnership is a fantastic way to start. It may take seeking out a new provider if you feel someone is not fit or taking your input seriously. You are capable and responsible for making the best choices about care options for your loved one.

In certain circumstances, you may find it necessary to get a second or third opinion to find the answers you need. A good physician should never be concerned about a patient seeking a second opinion or more information. If they are acting insulted or offended, it is in your best interest to ask yourself why. Both caregiver and care recipient must continue to seek the information needed to make the most informed decisions.

In your rapport with care providers, it is vitally important to have clear communication and to ask effective questions. A good first step is to be specific and concise by clearly stating your issue or question without getting mired down in unnecessary details. Rambling on or going into minute details that are not relevant does not move you further. Time is a commodity for providers and for you. When you simply and effectively share information, the professionals you are working with can quickly understand your concerns and give correct answers.

Also using open-ended questions can give you more detailed responses. Rather than asking, "Is the treatment plan effective?" you might ask, "Can you please explain the treatment plan?" Preparing in advance is also a terrific way to make sure you get the answers you need and make the best use of your time with a provider. Writing down questions and concerns before your appointment can help you remember what you intended to ask, especially if you often find yourself overwhelmed during appointments. This can be especially true if you are there with your child. In my experience, it was more difficult to manage when I had Isaac with me during appointments.

It can be helpful to bring someone with you to keep track of answers and be a support in these situations. Also, most smart phones now include a voice recording function, so requesting to record an appointment can help you relax in knowing you won't miss or forget anything and can relisten to what was said later. Sometimes you may not be processing all that is being said because of the emotional aspect of the situation. Learning new results or hearing difficult information adds other layers to your ability to take in all that is being shared. It may even be possible to email your questions to a provider or message them before the appointment, so they have time to reflect before the appointment.

Once a care provider has answered your question, it's helpful to repeat the answer in your own words. This allows the provider to clarify and helps to avoid misunderstandings or misinformation. Visit summaries have come a long way since I started this journey, and it is easier than ever to be in closer contact with medical providers.

Utilize all the tools at your disposal to build a collaborative relationship with all those who may be part of a care team: doctors, nurses, educators, therapists, or anyone else. When you approach these conversations as a partner with respect for the professional's ability while also valuing your role and knowledge of the needs of the care recipient, you will develop mutual respect, clear communication, and better outcomes for all involved.

Managing Emotions through Responsive Communication

It can be difficult to manage the emotions of a situation and refrain from making rash decisions based on how you feel in the moment. Taking the opportunity to practice responsive versus reactive communication fosters a better working relationship and keeps your name off the naughty list. We all know those people who manage to get their needs met but not productively or appropriately. When you are angry and aggressive, you are not putting your best foot forward, and trust me, while you may get what you want in the moment, it does not lend itself to productive relationships moving forward.

Sitting with your emotions and letting the dust settle allows you to adjust and come to a clearer choice with a cooler head. You may feel differently once you have had time to process away from the intensity of a situation. This is helpful when you can take the proper time and space for that.

Sometimes the luxury of processing time is not always available, and at these points it is especially helpful to trust those who are there to support you and your loved ones. Cooler heads than yours may prevail, so allow others to support you especially when you are feeling close to the breaking point. Managing your emotions can help reduce the stress of caregiving and enable you to provide better care. When you have the time to gather yourself and your composure, you can weigh your options objectively and make decisions that are in the best interest of all parties.

I found this difficult after my brain injury as it seemed my emotions were always raw and close to the surface. It was helpful for me to simply name it and claim it. I found no shame in sharing with others that I had a traumatic brain injury and was doing my absolute best to still be calm and engaged. I also shared this so that I would be given the time I needed to process information and exactly what was being said to me. Being open about your feelings and your challenges levels the playing field and encourages empathy in situations where you may be overwhelmed.

Taking some deep breaths, getting a drink of cool water, and having a moment of mindfulness do not hurt either. Keep those self-care skills at the ready so you can manage difficult emotions and avoid the negative impacts of chronic stress. Resiliency is necessary as you may be in the space of caregiving for a long time, and this foundational skill builds effective caregiving and advocacy.

Assertive communication allows you to balance respect for yourself with respect for others. It allows you to avoid vague statements and to be precise about what you want and what you are trying to express. Being specific and direct helps you avoid being misunderstood and extends far beyond interactions with professionals.

Avoid gross generalizations such as, "You always expect me to do everything." Such a statement might come across better as, "I'm feeling overwhelmed by all the tasks I have to do every day." Taking ownership of your feelings instead of slipping into the blame-and-shame game helps you stay in connection with others in your life. Caregiving includes layers of emotion and stress and taking responsibility for your feelings instead of passing blame on a loved one or care provider makes daily life easier and helps strengthen your relationships at a time when you most need support.

Tone of voice and body language are also important when situations are stressful. Have you ever interacted with someone with crossed arms, a scowl on their face, and a raised voice? How did that feel in comparison to interacting in a normal conversational tone with a relaxed posture? Stress and anxiety are rampant in caregiving. If we decrease stress and stay calm and composed by relaxing our body and managing our voice, it helps us have clarity and be able to listen to what is being said versus responding to nonverbal cues.

I often find myself speaking louder than I need to. When I realize this, I take a deep breath and lower the tone of my voice, and my body relaxes automatically. The same can happen to you. Having empathy and confirming the other person's viewpoint as you listen to understand strengthens your understanding of their situation and fosters respect. All too often we are listening to respond and not truly listening. It is helpful to repeat what you heard or ask for clarification if you are confused. Relationships built on positive and healthy communication strengthen trust and understanding and help us to focus on what is important.

Using Documentation to Improve Advocacy

Another helpful tool in developing advocacy is documentation. When you have carefully and completely documented your journey and the steps you have already taken, it lends credibility to your experience. Taking the time to track and check where you have been helps to remove roadblocks and wrong turns as you move forward. This increases your competency and builds confidence in sharing your understanding of the care needs.

Knowledge is powerful and you know your journey best of all. Having it documented is simply a way to share your knowledge and move the process forward more effectively. I remember when I would go with my dad to his medical appointments, and he would introduce me as his secretary. He always got a chuckle out of the provider, and it created an understanding between me and the provider that someone was there to support my dad. They realized he had added help and because I was there with records, they received a detailed understanding of where we had been and where we were going as it related to my dad's health goals.

When I first started my caregiving journey, I took copious notes and had binders filled with appointment information, medication lists and changes, providers' names, addresses, and phone numbers, and any number of Individual Education Plans and evaluation reports at the ready. Even after my accident, I kept all of my "homework" and activities in folders so I could do my job of recovering. You can use any number of systems, devices, apps, and tools that you find useful. The purpose is the same regardless of the form, and documentation allows you to improve care quality and communicate information to your healthcare providers and other care team members.

Learning to Navigate Systems and Programs

There are systems you must learn to navigate based on the individual needs and complexities of your care recipient. I was fortunate in my journey as a parent of a child with special needs to be a practicing speech-language pathologist who had experienced medical and educational systems. I also happened to practice within the early childhood special education system, in which Isaac participated beginning at 16 weeks of age. I knew the ins and outs of the system and advocating for the needs of my students for years helped me significantly as I navigated this same system as a parent.

Having a knowledge base of medical systems, terms, and conditions also gave me a leg up when I was my father's support and caregiver. It came full circle when I needed to work through similar systems following my accident, which was the most difficult for me. I was far more able to work effectively for others than for myself. This is another reason why it is so important to develop a skill set as a caregiver as you never know when the tables may turn, and you will need to advocate for yourself. Even if you do not have the skills in this space to begin with, there are ways to learn and acquire them and we will address those later in this chapter.

Every system you interact with has its nuances and complexities and it is not necessary to know everything about each one. It can be helpful to have at least a base of knowledge about the way specific programs work. Knowing even basic information about insurance plans, educational documents, and common terms makes you feel more secure in new environments.

Every agency and program have a unique list of terms and acronyms which can be confusing to the uninitiated. Don't be afraid to ask for clarification. Often, these professionals may not even be aware of the number of things they are saying which make no sense to someone new to the situation, simply because it is so commonplace for them. This may be a good time to ask for support. Insurance companies may have a navigator, or a clinic may have a care manager or coordinator available to help you.

Educational advocacy groups are also useful for assistance, and they may even have volunteers or paid staff who will attend meetings with you. It is useful to ask questions about who may be able to help you. Asking other caregivers can be a wonderful way to find help and develop more skills. If you find someone whom you connect with or who is particularly helpful, keep their name and contact information available.

I also think it is helpful to take the additional step of letting supervisors or systems know when someone has gone out of their way to support you. Being able to give a shoutout increases the likelihood that behavior and support will continue which will help you and increase better outcomes for other caregivers in the same system. It takes a village, and we all need to be in the mindset of raising expectations and advocating not only for our specific situation but for the greater good of all in need. Systems have evolved over the years based on feedback from others, highlighting the importance of advocacy in driving systemic changes for better care for all.

Once again, it is important to document calls and interactions along with specific names if possible. In this way, you can effectively and efficiently communicate your needs, which raises the potential for greater success. Track the time, date, and who you spoke to and the details of your call or interaction. The time spent will be well worth it, especially if you have challenges in getting your needs met. You will be able to come back with specific information and a "paper trail" that can help in finding out who was involved and what was the last point of contact. It takes time up front but is extremely helpful overall.

When I think back on many of the lessons I learned from advocating and setting up effective communication, I think the biggest one was I felt empowered. I learned that my firsthand experiences mattered, and I was reinforced when I spoke up about questions, concerns, and issues. I realized that I knew exactly what my life lessons had been, and no one could argue with my life experiences. Sharing those experiences with other parents, both personally and professionally, helped keep the momentum moving forward for all of us.

If assertive communication is not your go-to, take the opportunity to get training. Advocacy groups – including disability rights advocates, family support groups, or groups related to a specific diagnosis – often offer workshops or training sessions that can help you to grow your skill set. You can even practice assertive communication in front of a mirror or with a trusted friend. Learning to be responsive versus reactive in new or uncomfortable situations goes a long way toward a higher level of engagement with others.

Also, if this is a strong area for you, consider sharing your skills and experiences with others for the greater good of all. Take the helpful information and leave what is not. Realize that no one knows your family's needs and situation better than you do. Own your story and let your voice be heard because you are the only one who can share your unique experiences. If you don't feel supported by a provider, organization, or educator, speak up. You never know how many others are feeling the same way and are afraid to let someone know.

When you approach situations with curiosity instead of judgment, you can remove the emotion from a situation and potentially improve relationships by preventing conflict and misunderstandings. You can also consider seeking out a coach or mentor to build your advocacy skills or as a sounding board.

We all have different traits and talents. When your caregiving journey begins you may be worried that you will not be able to sustain this lifestyle or manage all day-to-day challenges. Understand that you can promote your strengths and build abilities in areas that need to be developed. Remember your voice has power. Advocacy and clear effective communication are not only skills but tools you can use to transform the quality of care your loved ones receive and other areas of your personal and professional life. Your role as a caregiver is invaluable.

Every question you ask and each time you look for understanding, you are contributing to better care. Embrace this space of growth and knowledge. Build both formal and informal support networks to help you continue advocating for the people you love and care for. Caregivers must remain in community with one another so they can all continue to thrive with the care and respect they deserve. Step forward bravely with strength, compassion, and resilience as you use the power of advocacy and clear communication to enhance the care for those you love.

CHAPTER 6:
Chapter Questions and Workbook

Reflection Questions:

What do you think about when the word advocacy comes to mind? How have you had to advocate for yourself and your care recipient? Do you feel comfortable speaking up for yourself? Are you able to ask questions of healthcare providers, educators, and others who are a part of your caregiving journey? What does advocacy look like for you?

Journal Prompts:

- Reflect on a recent conversation in which you advocated for the care needs of your loved one.

_____

_____

_____

_____

_____

- What were your main concerns and how did you express them? Did you feel understood by the other person? What, if anything, would you do in future conversations to ensure clearer communication?

_____

- Think about a time when you found it difficult to communicate your needs or boundaries as a caregiver.

- What emotions did you experience? What were the challenges you met with in expressing your needs? How can you build your confidence to communicate more effectively in similar situations in the future?

Action Steps:

Below you will find a diagram for effective communication techniques.

With these tips in mind work through a current communication challenge and brainstorm potential solutions.

Example: I feel angry with my partner over unequal caregiving duties.

Potential solutions: Instead of choosing not to express myself, I can prepare my thoughts and concerns and ask for time to sit down and talk. I will ask open-ended questions such as, "How are you feeling about the care duties we share?" I will give specific examples rather than use words like always or never and say, "When I am home all day caring for _____, I feel frustrated when you come home late." Effective communication takes practice so give yourself some grace as you process through it.

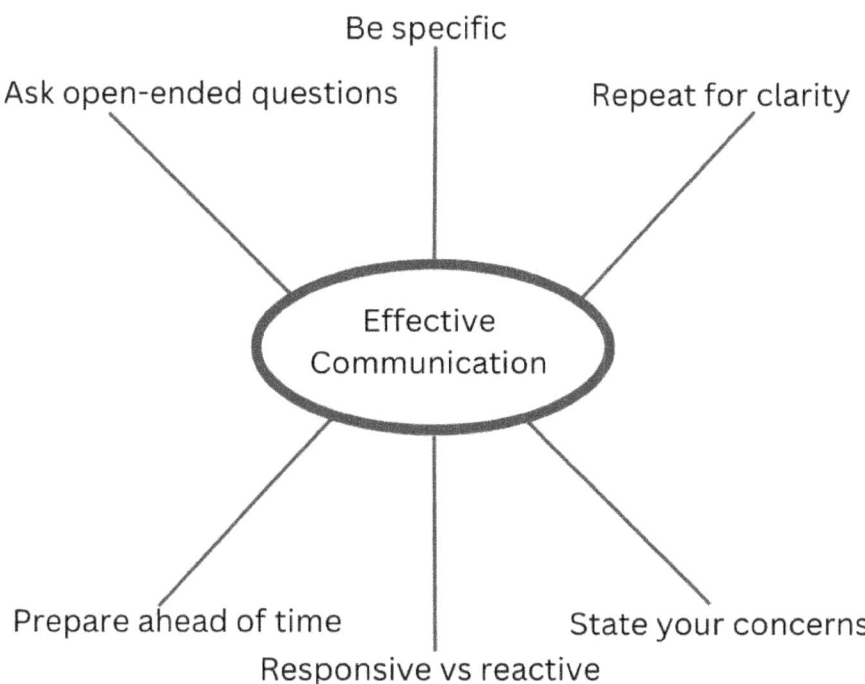

"Little by little, one travels far." — J.R.R. Tolkien

CHAPTER 7:
Small Victories and Milestones

Everyone has a journey with a different number of steps. Life is about not only the big moments but also the moments that make a difference in many ways. For caregivers, recognizing and celebrating even the smallest victories is crucial on this often long and winding road. This may be the most important wisdom I have gained in my experience as a caregiver and my recovery as well.

It first became clear to me when Isaac was discharged from the hospital, and I was coming to terms with all that had happened and how very quickly life had changed. Typical development went out the window and it was time for a complete mind shift. With my first child, it was all about when she was going to roll over, sit up, or crawl. I knew these actions were going to occur and it was just a question of the timeline. In typical new parent fashion, one milestone was met, quickly celebrated, and announced, and we were looking ahead to the next step and ready to achieve success.

There was truly little thought or expectation as to how it would happen; it just did. When Isaac came along all those givens were gone. I was hopeful that he would grow and develop to the best of his abilities, and I felt incredibly responsible for ensuring that would come to be. Whereas in the past it had been normal to place my daughter on a blanket to play, there were now new protocols and meanings.

There were specific positions for play and recommendations for the best toys for small babies with blindness and with cerebral palsy. Instead of going to the toy section and simply grabbing a brightly colored item, it became a research project to find which objects had the best sensory input and how he would interact with them. I can tell you more than once Isaac's "toys" were sourced from household items, pet toys, and craft supplies from the local dollar store.

I would stand in the aisle with my eyes closed to fully immerse myself in Isaac's world as best I could. I am sure people were wondering what I was doing. His best toy was a cardboard box turned upside down as his "little room." We hung items from the top and sides and whenever he moved, he touched something new. The concept of this little room, designed for infants with blindness or children with severe disabilities to interact with their environment, is part of the Active Learning Space approach for blind children developed by Dr. Lilli Nielsen.

Understanding that he needed to learn about space and distance and early object awareness uniquely, having this safe space around him allowed him to begin to learn about his environment. His big sister, Brenna, would lie on the floor with him for hours and explore. What a wonderful thing it was to see this bonding and sibling attachment along with his ability to reach out and know there was something beyond himself. I saw this as a huge milestone and victory to celebrate. It was not sitting up or rolling over, but Isaac was learning, and he was curious about the world. We just had to find a way to help him access it differently. This is a good lesson to learn as caregivers. Our world is not less than, it is simply different.

When we approach change and new challenges with curiosity instead of concern, we open our eyes to innumerable ways to learn and victories to celebrate.

As the day-to-day changed and the crisis level of functioning decreased, it was time to settle into the new journey of caregiving beyond motherhood. Instead of playgroups, Isaac had visits from therapists and teachers, and they became my connection points as well. Everything seemed to revolve around Isaac but in reality, we were all also adjusting to a new normal.

Acknowledging and Celebrating Effort, Progress, and Victories

After six months of intervention and significant practice, Isaac rolled over for the first time and I can tell you, it was worth celebrating. Taking the time to recognize all the effort that goes into achieving milestones is a wonderful way to confirm your steps and efforts. Soak it in and acknowledge your part in the achievement. Taking the time to celebrate helps keep you motivated and shows appreciation for the hard work and dedication involved in caregiving. When you savor a victory dopamine is released, and you receive a nice boost of positive emotions. These positive emotions affect not only you but your care recipient as well. It helps you to build momentum to achieve the next milestone and gives you a point to focus on.

Celebrating is a way to positively reinforce yourself and acknowledge your progress. When you take time to notice and appreciate what you have achieved and learned, you begin to see added possibilities ahead. Celebrating your successes helps you realize your potential and sets you up for more ambitious goals in the future. The celebrations boost your confidence and help you appreciate the skills you have gained. All the enjoyment and satisfaction that come with celebrating lets you propel yourself forward to achieve other goals and prevents burnout by focusing on the positive moments of your experiences in caregiving. This is a win for both care partners – the caregiver and care recipient.

In caregiving situations, you may have distinct types of goals. Your loved one may have a terminal illness or dementia, and he or she is not necessarily going to be making progress toward specific goals in the way a young child might. You can still celebrate joint accomplishments of finding a substitute caregiver, accessing resources you have needed, or even celebrating when you have a medication that is helping with fewer side effects. For someone living with life-altering conditions or disabilities, even small achievements and victories can hold a great deal of significance.

For me, being able to shower independently and style my hair led me to feel a great deal of joy. Realizing all the things I took for granted as an able-bodied individual gives me endless opportunities for gratitude. Celebrations of victories and milestones are a wonderful way to normalize your life as it looks now. Turn the practice of celebrating your wins into a habit and a normal aspect of life. Wouldn't the world be so much happier if we focused on celebrating rather than getting bogged down by negative self-talk and discontent? Celebrating the moments as they came and not waiting or expecting the next step was helpful.

We can accept our challenges more easily if we can also find joy in the journey. There is a wonderful book by BJ Fogg, *Tiny Habits: The Small Changes That Change Everything*. In it, he sums up the importance of celebration. "Celebration is the best way to create a positive feeling that wires in your new habits. It's free, fast, and available to people of every color, shape, size, income, and personality. In addition, celebration teaches us to be nice to ourselves – a skill that pays out the biggest dividends of all."

Fun ideas for celebrating small caregiving wins could be:

- Keeping a journal of when you have an "aha moment" or good day. Remember, progress is never too small to celebrate. Being able to look back and see these shining moments is a wonderful way to document your journey and joint accomplishments.

- Create a "warm fuzzy file" to keep cards or notes of encouragement you may have received. You can include quotes that are inspirational to you as well. I scan cards from friends or texts I receive and keep them on my phone. If I am having a distressing day, they are a wonderful way to encourage myself and remind me of my inherent value.

- Take the opportunity to let someone know when you have a positive update or even a good day. It may not look like a social media moment, but it doesn't need to. Family and friends want to encourage us and one of the best ways is to share our wins no matter how small they may seem. This creates the community support you need to keep going on the tough days.

- Allow yourself to celebrate even challenging tasks. Getting through a difficult medical appointment or a meeting with a school individualized education program (IEP) team is a perfect time to treat yourself. I honestly celebrated when I made it through a school meeting without crying. It took me until Isaac was 20 to achieve that one.

- Practicing self-care is a great celebration and it does not have to break the bank. Taking a walk with a friend, pouring a cup of tea or your beverage of choice, or reading a few pages in a book or magazine can be a way to nurture yourself and soak in gratitude for what you have done.

- Make sure to include your loved one in the celebration. Use words of affirmation for the effort you are both putting in to make progress and do not expect perfection.

- Include the whole family and have a progress party. Let everyone choose one win they had for the week and pick a unique way to celebrate. A pizza party or a game night would be a way to celebrate everyone's progress. This is a fun time for siblings who may feel left out in the busyness of caregiving.

The journey of caregiving has considerable difficulties, and it has multiple rewards as well. What may have seemed like a negative situation at one point in time can have positive implications as you continue down the caregiving road. We can only see through the window we are currently looking out. Allowing yourself the time to appreciate where you started, and your forward momentum is good for both your mental and physical well-being. Never miss the chance to celebrate.

As you look back on the wins you have had along the way, find continued motivation and acknowledge the progress you have made. Validating your dedication and hard work as a caregiver is important for your resilience and positive well-being. Caregiving may be part of your life for a brief period or a lifetime and your mental health matters. Finding the space to be proud of the care you provide and the effort you put in is essential in recognizing your inherent value in the caregiving space.

Defining Goals and Challenges

It is also important to define what new goals and challenges await you. As you look ahead in your journey you will find goal setting for the long-term course requires a clear plan and specific goals to strive toward. Planning the next steps and having a clear course forward are important to sustaining progress over time. Progress may not necessarily be linear. In chronic caregiving situations, it may be cyclical.

I experienced this when caring for my father. He would have a fall or need a short-term hospital stay often followed by a rehabilitation period in a transitional care setting. This is a frequent situation for individuals caring for an aging or ill parent or care recipient. This can become exhausting for both parties, which is why it is important to have a clear understanding of the next steps. Knowing the current condition of the care recipient before a change of status gives you a point to strive for. If you do not know where your loved one was functioning before a change in condition, it can be difficult to figure out future needs and a plan as you move forward.

Setting goals is an essential part of reaching the milestones or outcomes we hope to achieve, whether those goals are for ourselves as caregivers or for our care partner. I always appreciate seeing caregivers set goals to prioritize self-care. I know from experience it is hard to put yourself at the top of the list as a caregiver. Honestly, sometimes it is hard to even make the list or see it in the distance. Some people are noticeably confident and used to setting goals for themselves. For others of you, this will be a completely new endeavor. It is useful to know why goals are important if you want to achieve a particular goal.

Goals are particularly significant for caregivers and care recipients:

1. They provide direction and purpose. When you are in a space of caring for another, it is helpful to know the result you want. What is it you are specifically trying to achieve? What are you working toward? Are you trying to alleviate symptoms? Are you trying to practice a specific skill? Are you trying to find more balance in your life? Are you trying to prioritize your own health needs? If you have clearly defined goals, you know more about your direction, which can help you feel more in control of what often feels like an uncontrollable situation.

2. Goals provide motivation and engagement. Having something defined to work toward can help both care partners stay engaged in the caregiving journey. As we discussed earlier it is helpful to have milestones to celebrate. Goals we work toward and achieve provide a sense of validation and accomplishment on a sometimes-thankless journey. They also encourage you to continue to progress for your greater good.

3. Goals are important for person-centered care. Encouraging the care recipient to be a part of goal setting can increase self-esteem and self-confidence and can validate their thoughts on the journey. It is crucial to consider the desires of the person receiving care. I have seen situations in which family members – albeit well-meaning – leave the person receiving care completely out of the discussion on their own care goals. We must always assume competency and begin the

discussions of desired outcomes with the person who is going to be receiving care. This is another place where curiosity is a great approach. Rather than directing the other person or telling them what is going to happen or be done to them, consider curiosity. Consider asking the question, "I'm curious what your thoughts are about this treatment?" or "I'm curious what goals you may have for your physical therapy sessions?" Self-advocacy itself may be the goal and including the care recipient in the journey builds skills in this area.

4. Goals are needed to measure progress. If you don't have any goal to measure, how will you know when you are progressing? The effectiveness of care plans and treatments cannot be accurately checked if we don't have a framework for measuring progress. Being able to track improvements and setbacks allows you to change and adjust your care accordingly. Being able to note progress is a way to measure the care recipient's overall satisfaction and well-being.

5. Goals provide a sense of empowerment and independence. When we encourage care recipients to take part in and set their own goals, we are showing that we value their input. We recognize them as partners in care. Of course, this may not be possible for everyone but, if possible, encourage those receiving care to make choices toward goals for better quality of life and satisfaction with care.

6. Goals can help better communication and collaboration with care team partners. When you set up goals and relay them to others on your care team there can be increased collaboration. When everyone is on the same page about what needs to be done, care is likely to be better coordinated and more effective. Also, working together on a common goal solidifies the team as a unit which increases the overall effectiveness of the care team.

Knowing why goals are important in caregiving is a good starting point. Now let's move on to figure out the steps in setting a goal and work through the process of turning an idea into a measurable goal. A wonderful way to begin is to decide what it is you are looking to achieve.

I always encourage caregivers to have at least one goal for self-care. The goal is to get more exercise, have more social connections with friends, or take time for yourself on a regular basis. No matter what you choose for the overarching goal it is helpful to break it into smaller sub-goals or milestones.

If you start with the final step and work backward, moving through each preceding step until you reach the beginning, you're using a method called backward planning. Moving backward to the first step gives you a road map to achieving your goal. Then you can put it into focused, actionable steps. In caregiving and in life, goal setting can be a fantastic way to achieve your best outcomes. If you don't know what you are trying to achieve, it can feel like you have no momentum and cause you to feel hopeless in trying times.

Using the SMART Method of Goal Setting

One of the best ways to move forward with goals is to make sure the goals you are setting are SMART. This concept was developed in 1981 by George T. Doran. SMART stands for specific, measurable, achievable, relevant, and time-focused. If this is a new concept for you here is a brief description. Let's process.

- **SPECIFIC** – Goals with more details are specific, which makes them more effective. If you simply state, "I want to see my friends more often," it is just a broad statement. By changing it to, "I want to see my friends once per week," it adds specific details and starts the goal-setting process.

- **MEASURABLE** – A goal of seeing friends "more often" is not measurable. You want to see them more often than what?

How often do you see them now? Having a baseline allows you to make your goal measurable. Seeing your friends once a week is measurable and can easily be tracked on a calendar.

- **ACHIEVABLE** – Look at what is currently going on in your life. This can help you decide if this is an achievable goal for you. You want to have something to strive for, but is this a true possibility for you? Will you have caregiving backup in order to see your friends weekly? Do you need to plan for substitute caregivers? If it doesn't seem achievable it may make more sense to set a more realistic goal. Perhaps twice a month makes more sense as a starting point. You want to feel your goal is something you can achieve, or it is unlikely you will reach it.

- **RELEVANT** – Is this something that makes sense for you in your life? The goal should be relevant to what you are trying to achieve, which in this case is more social connections with friends. It should serve a purpose for you and move you closer to your desired outcome, which is to increase your engagement and decrease isolation.

- **TIME-FOCUSED** – There should be a specific timeline, so that you know whether you have met the goal or made progress toward it. In our example, we are talking about seeing friends once a week or maybe twice a month. To make your goal time-focused, you need an end date or due date. How long will it take before you can achieve getting together with friends? Will you know if you have achieved it if you connect with friends twice a month for each of the next three months? Decide what makes sense for your current lifestyle to allow for a timeline that works.

Action Planning

As we walk through the SMART goal process you can see we have taken the idea of wanting to get together with friends from a vague idea into a more structured and detailed goal. Rather than an open-ended idea or wish, we have taken steps to plan. The goal has now become: "I want to get together with friends twice a month for each of the next three months." This is a specific, measurable, achievable, relevant, and time-focused plan.

The next part of the process is using the backward planning process to develop an action plan. Action plans are the steps we need to take in order to make the goal a reality. Let's move our social connection goal into the action planning process for some more practice.

I have broken action planning down into something I call "The Five P's of Action Planning".

The first **P** is for **Plan**. We need to have a plan in place so that we can begin working toward our goal. What might our plan look like? Well, first you probably need to reach out to a friend to set up a time to get together; this may be step one in your plan. So, you will go step-by-step through your plan to decide what you need to do to achieve your goals.

Our next **P** is **Prioritize**. To take the first steps, you need to make it a priority. I think of it as a seed habit. A seed habit is the tiniest step you take to make the first working step toward your goal. If you think about it in layers, once you have the first seed planted then you go forward and move to the next one and eventually those seeds are going to sprout.

Our third **P** is for **Persevere**. Being a caregiver can be challenging because things come up and change quickly. Those roadblocks sometimes get in the way of us getting out and doing the things we want to do. It can be helpful to think ahead to what those challenges or roadblocks might be. Maybe one of the roadblocks might be the illness of a family member or the care recipient. There could be harsh weather, or a caregiver might have to cancel. Many things could happen. Then you might think what can I do to be ready for a roadblock? For example, if your substitute caregiver can't come, maybe you could invite your friend over to your house instead of going out. Granted it may not be as exciting as going out but at least you get a chance to visit with a friend and you are still taking care of your social needs.

Next, we have a **P** for Progress. You want to make sure you are making progress toward your goal and following your action plan. If it's been two weeks and you haven't taken any steps to get together with a friend, you are probably not making much progress. Keeping that in mind and checking your progress will help you in achieving your goals and taking better care of yourself.

Our final **P** is **Partner**, which is one of my favorites. You need to find people who can help you be accountable to take care of yourself. Whether this is a family member or friend or even a coach, having someone who helps you follow through on the steps to promote self-care or any type of goal you want to achieve is particularly important. Having someone there to back you up, encourage you, and tell you it is OK to take a break is valuable in setting goals. We sometimes need the validation of another person to remind us we don't need to earn self-care.

Take Care of Yourself

Self-care is not a reward. It is a responsibility to yourself.

Once again, I want to remind you to honor yourself in the often-complicated caregiving equation. You must prioritize your own self-care to keep up the physical, mental, and emotional strength to continue to care for others in need. Setting goals supports you and your care partner and encourages you to take care of yourself during caregiving.

It is also important on this journey of milestones and victories to find your cheerleaders. Who are the ones who lift you up and support you on even the darkest of days, the friendly faces you can always turn to and who buoy you up when days are hard? It can become easy to lose our way when so much time, energy, and effort go into caring for others.

So often we speak to ourselves in a way that is unkind. We have expectations of ourselves we would never hold for another. We think about ourselves in ways we would never think of others. That internal dialogue can become our harshest critic, so practice speaking to yourself with love and compassion for the journey that has come to you. We often move into the caregiving space not by choice but by necessity.

Finding in yourself a space for self-love, self-compassion, and encouragement is a gift, not only to yourself but also to your care recipient. They also want to see you thrive as a caregiver. Allow them to celebrate you and all the amazing contributions you bring as you develop your caregiving toolbox. Everyone will have their own journey. Your role is to make your journey the absolute best possible and to acknowledge and accept that you are just one person trying to make your way in what feels like a whole new world. It is important to take the time to develop your skills and stay present in the moment-by-moment spaces.

Don't be afraid to pat yourself on the back for staying on the course and to release the expectations of perfection. It is unnecessary to negate our accomplishments or our progress. Celebrate every chance you get because you deserve it and so do the people in your life. Don't let the "should monster" eat away at you and leave you stuck in a cycle of shame and guilt. Be proud of what you do every day for those you love and care for. Remember not to compare your insides to someone else's outsides as everyone has milestones that look different. Don't let negative thoughts, beliefs, or actions take you away from the incredibly important work you are doing as a caregiver. Don't allow fear to fuel you. Find joy in your journey and rejoice in the celebrations unique to you. Allow yourself to celebrate the day-to-day victories as you continue to set goals and gain skills in this new world of caregiving.

CHAPTER 7:
Chapter Questions and Workbook

Reflection Questions:

What milestones have you celebrated in your lifetime? Have you set SMART goals before? What goals have you accomplished and how did it feel when you were successful? Have you thought about self-care as an area for improvement? Who are your strongest supporters?

Journal Prompts:

- Think about the past week or month in your caregiving journey. What small victories or milestones did you achieve, either for yourself or the person you are caring for? How did you feel about them? What steps did you take to reach them?

_____

_____

_____

_____

_____

- As you reflect on goal setting, what is one area of self-care you have been neglecting? What is a small step you can take forward toward achieving a goal for self-care? Who might support you in reaching this goal?

_____

_____

_____

_____

_____

Action Steps:

Create a warm, fuzzy file for yourself. Save encouraging messages from the people who support you or find quotes or photographs that keep you focused on the positive.

Set a SMART goal for yourself based on a self-care need you currently have. Use the prompts below to help you reach the goal.

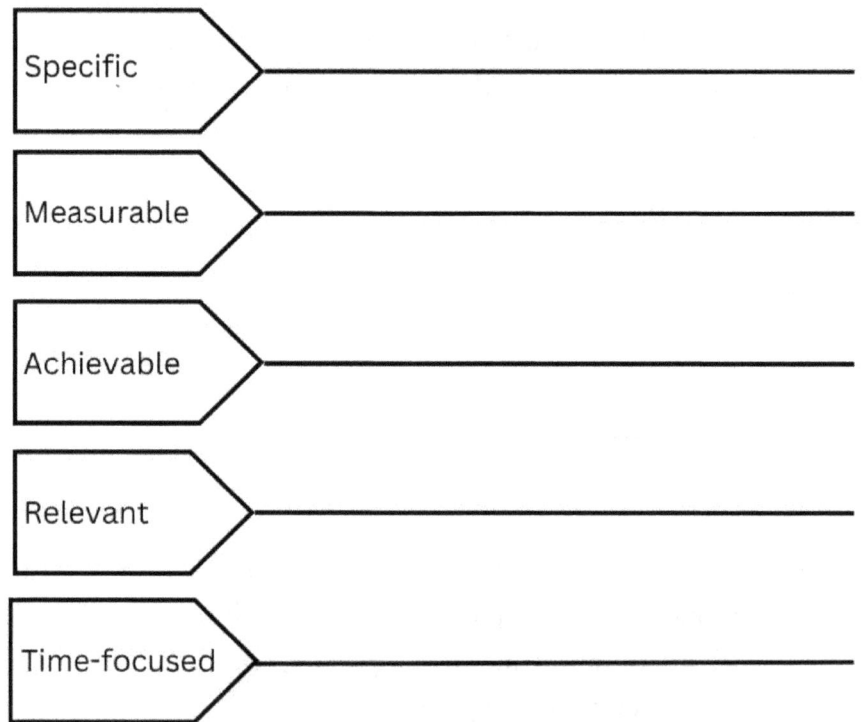

"By failing to prepare, you are preparing to fail". — Benjamin Franklin

CHAPTER 8:
Long-term Caregiving and Adaptation

I vividly remember the night Isaac was born. Brenna was four and had chickenpox. Since I needed all possible days for my parental leave, I asked my parents to come and watch her before the baby came. They had just arrived, and we were sitting down to dinner and having a lively conversation when, by surprise, my water broke. My mother was insistent that I should head to the hospital at once, but I assured her we had time, and I wanted to finish my meal.

Her concern was palpable as she was remembering the trauma of R.C.'s birth and death the previous year. She had only survived 18 hours before she left us. My parents never even met her nor did any other family members. She was like a butterfly who flitted into and out of our lives on a breeze, yet she had stayed a constant in our hearts and souls.

Given this challenge in my recent past, my mother was not sure it was the best idea to delay. I felt differently, and after a change of clothing, I finished my dinner, and my husband and I headed to the hospital. We arrived around 7 p.m., and within just three hours, Isaac James had made his appearance. He was perfect, and it felt as if life was turning around. I hoped the pain and loss of R.C. would now fade and it would be time to turn a corner and start down a different path. Little did we know how soon the tides would turn again and we would be in another space we had never wanted to enter – the "forever space" where caring for another lasts a lifetime.

When I returned to work after about two months of parental leave, I looked at the quote of the day calendar on my desk. While removing the days that had already passed, I found the quote from Isaac's birth date, by Earl Nightingale: "Never give up on a dream just because of the time it will take to accomplish it. The time will pass anyway." I thought this was a wonderful quote and I took it home and put it in a frame on Isaac's bedroom wall. I had no idea the impact this quote would have on the rest of my life.

I believe losing R.C. prepared me for the journey with Isaac. I knew the pain of losing my daughter and even with all the heartache that came with Isaac's illness, I felt immense gratitude for having him with us. Once I knew Isaac was going to survive, it was time to adapt to the fact that I would be a caregiver for the rest of either Isaac's life or my own.

The idea in the quote of "never giving up on a dream because of the time it will take" resonates with the challenges and perseverance needed for long-term caregiving. Caring for a loved one over an extended period can feel like an endless journey at times. There are times when you want to get off the merry-go-round and yearn for a life with fewer struggles and heartache. I wanted a child who would grow up and thrive and have endless opportunities for fulfillment and independence. I wanted Isaac's life to be easy – every parent's dream.

Isaac's life is rife with options for fulfillment and joy. He smiles with his whole being and has a laugh that makes everyone smile. That seems right because the meaning of the name Isaac is "he will laugh." Biblically, Isaac was a miracle to his parents, Abraham and Sarah, who were far too old to have children. Our Isaac is also a miracle. This boy who grew older but never grew up is still sweet, innocent, and childlike. He has goals to achieve, and growth has continued for him on his timeline. He brightens my world in endless ways, and I am forever grateful to be his mom.

This quote also encourages us to keep up hope and commitment in the caregiving role, despite how daunting the time may seem. For the "time will pass anyway" is also quite relevant. Whether being a short-term or long-term caregiver is one you easily adapt to or struggle with, time will still march on. Realizing this new normal is the loss of a dream or a belief in how life was supposed to look. Grief will be a part of the process and adapting to change is part of that too. Dreams can change and look different at different viewing points. Realizing your timeline has changed from finite points to being open-ended can be discouraging.

The Necessity of Learning to Plan and Adapt in Long-term Caregiving

Staying dedicated to caregiving as the years go by is a process of adaptation. Adapting to the life changes and new normal of a long-term caregiving situation requires tremendous patience, resilience, and a refusal to surrender one's aspirations for their loved one's well-being. Different, not less than, is truly an attitude to hold and uphold as a long-term caregiver. Staying steadfast in your mindset is a necessity for your health and well-being as you enter the long-term caregiving space.

It is normal and necessary to take time to realize this new normal is different than you expected. Allowing yourself to grieve the loss and changes and what you believed life would be is important. Take your time, process, heal, break down, and repeat. The journey continues and it is necessary to allow yourself to be wherever you are in any given moment, for the time will pass anyway. I realize now how important this step is, so I strive to encourage others to find the space to grieve and process the difficult emotions that come with loss and change.

In my own life, it took me an exceptionally long time – decades in fact to process through the grief and loss that occurred in my life. I was thrust so quickly into primary caregiving that there was no time to process. Not only did I not have time to process what had happened to Isaac, I had not had time to process the death of R.C. When she died, I was distraught and broken and then within 4 months, I was pregnant again with Isaac. Not only did I not have the time to reflect and grieve but physically my body had been through so much. Two pregnancies, the death of a child, and another child in a life threatening and life altering situation all occurred within a 22-month period. When I think about it now, I am not sure how I even functioned or found my way through this time. It took me nearly 25 years and the help of a therapy practice called Accelerated Resolution Therapy to fully come to terms with both the loss of R.C. and the challenges Isaac encountered as an infant.

I encourage you to do better and find the care you need, either with personal support from family and friends or professional help to process all these intense emotions. It is not an easy task, but it is possible to find healing and move on in a new and healthier way.

You may have heard the expression, "People do not plan to fail, they fail to plan." This is all too common in the caregiving space because often the situations come about without warning. It is important to begin having conversations about aging, end-of-life wishes, and care options before caregiving is thrust upon you. No one wants to have these conversations, yet everyone needs to! Letting your loved ones know you want the best possible outcomes for their long-term health and well-being is one reason. Expressing your desire to support them in the ways they want to be supported is also important.

No one wants to be told what to do, so it is best to ask open-ended questions about their thoughts, hopes, and what they expect as they age. Rather than telling someone it is time to quit driving, try asking, "How comfortable are you feeling with driving?" or "What do you think about the traffic these days?" Sharing your own thoughts without directing their behavior is beneficial. Think about how you might want to have these conversations as you age.

It is a good reminder to have the same discussion with your children or future care partners at the same time. It is never too early to start preparing for caregiving. Also, explain to them that you want to follow their wishes and if you do not know what those wishes are it is difficult to comply. You can also share your concerns about balancing your life and having information before it is necessary is one way you can support your future goals and expectations. If the conversation is not going anywhere or there is resistance, it is OK to table it for the time being.

Keeping an atmosphere of openness and availability versus frustration and demands will lead to more positive outcomes and maintain an open and caring relationship. The goal is to be respectful and compassionate while taking the time you need to plan. You may need to have multiple conversations on the topic, which is another reason to start exploring your aging options early.

Assessing Financial Resources

It is beneficial to take the time to assess current financial resources and research the costs of care earlier than later. If you know up front what to expect you can plan accordingly, regardless of where you are in the process. Do you know your rights and the rights of the care recipient? If they have a specific disability, you may find someone who specializes in that area. What is in place in terms of healthcare directives and setting up a power of attorney? Do you know where all the information on finances and legal paperwork is stored? What banks or financial institutions are involved and what resources are available for care?

Taking the time to connect with a financial adviser or attorney is helpful in order to learn what options are available to you as you budget and plan for future care. Knowing how to protect your financial future, manage your money, and understand the costs of caregiving is a major step at this point. If you are caregiving for your child with disabilities, will you need to set up guardianship as they reach adulthood? Setting up a special needs trust to ensure your child will have access to all the things they may need when you are no longer here is a major step.

Caregiving can have a significant impact on your career, not only for the primary caregiver but for your care partner as well. The need for one person to carry the weight of all the financial needs of a family that had been supported by two full-time workers is intense. Isaac's dad took on the burden to be the primary breadwinner so I could take a full school year off to be home with Isaac. His ability to continue working in this manner was a gift many families are not able to access, either because of the types of jobs they hold or because they are single parents.

Another amazing thing that happened when Isaac got sick was that within days my work colleagues had donated their own sick days to cover my salary through the end of the school year in 1996. I have been incredibly blessed by co-workers in many ways and this was just one example. Because I carried the health insurance for our family, it was imperative that I return to work. By this time, Brenna, our daughter, was in kindergarten halftime, so we were able to save some childcare dollars, which helped us financially as well.

We had to be creative the next year as well. Because Isaac was now a child with a disability, we completed the process to apply for TEFRA. The TEFRA option (short for Tax Equity and Fiscal Responsibility Act, the federal law that set the rules for this option) provided medical assistance for children with disabilities who had families with incomes too high to qualify for standard medical assistance. We paid a premium to access this program, and Isaac's dad managed the financial needs of our family while I was out of work. By utilizing this program, we were able to have respite care for Isaac. Our good friend and Isaac's godmother, Jane, helped us out by providing this service to us. This, along with some creative scheduling options, and the support of my employer allowed me to return to work part time when Isaac was 20 months old. It was a juggling act for my spouse and I, and it took effort, but again, we kept it together and kept moving forward. Each year took cooperation between the two of us as we decided how we could manage the financial and daily needs of our family and the care of Isaac.

Because I carried the health insurance for our family, I had to return to my job full-time the following year when Isaac was almost three. I became one of the millions of caregivers who work outside the home and carry the burden of caregiving. So many people do not have the luxury of time off or careers that support options such as part-time or flexible employment. We will talk more about employer support for caregiving employees in Chapter 10. It remains a significant issue for working caregivers to this day and needs to be addressed as a global issue.

Knowledge is power and asking questions and advocating become even more crucial once you have crossed the threshold to long-term caregiving. What resources do you currently have which may supplement the costs of care? Do you have a long-term care insurance policy? What does it cover and how does it pay? Each policy is different in terms of what services are covered, and the process can be complicated. Reaching out to the long-term care insurance provider for an overview of a policy may save you any number of wrong turns as you plan.

Most policies have a 30-, 60-, or 90-day elimination period where you or your care recipient may have to pay out-of-pocket expenses. Knowing what the daily limit is can help you make a comparison on the costs of home-based care versus assisted living or memory care. Is your loved one eligible for state aid or Medicare? Is your loved one a veteran or did he or she complete military service? There may be added benefits available through the Veterans Administration. Dig deep to find available resources as there may be a much higher cost to caregiving than you expect. You need to protect your assets as well as those of your loved one. The best-case scenario is having discussions with your loved one before they are in the caregiving space. Unfortunately, this happens in a small percentage of families.

Assessing Physical and Emotional Abilities as a Caregiver

Beyond your financial resources, it is important to complete a check-in on your physical and emotional ability. Are you taking care of your own health? Be honest with yourself and your loved one as you evaluate your own physical abilities and limitations. After my accident, it was clear Isaac would need to transition to a new living situation sooner than we had planned on or expected. After collaborating with his social worker and visiting different options, Isaac moved from our home to a wonderful family foster care home when he was twenty-one. Even though I felt comfortable with the choice we made, it was exceedingly difficult to move Isaac out of our home. Because of his significant need for care, it felt a little like sending a toddler to college. Isaac has thrived in his new home, and we are blessed to have his foster care provider, Becky, on our team. Knowing he is well cared for gives me another opportunity to be grateful.

It is also imperative to take inventory of your emotional health. Are you finding time to prioritize your own mental health and well-being? You are the first line of defense as a caregiver and decreasing stress, building emotional resilience, and avoiding burnout are essential for your best life. Seeking professional help is one way to continue to build your emotional health, deal with the difficulties of caregiving, and improve your quality of life as you learn to acknowledge emotions without judgment. Having a coach or mental health professional who can help you process the changes in your life is a great asset. They may be involved in your life through many twists and turns.

Managing and caring for another person who needs long-term care can be very draining and there are times when you are going to feel overwhelmed, overworked, and simply exhausted. It is OK not to be OK. Asking for help is easier when you have thought ahead, have support systems in place, and are realistic about your own ability to be a long-term caregiver.

Finding Secondary and Outside Care Services

In long-term caregiving, it is important for families not to make promises that may be hard to keep. Telling mom or dad they will be able to stay at home forever is a wonderful thought and something we can all strive for, but it may not be possible. Home healthcare and secondary caregivers can be a great asset in helping folks age in place and for families in situations like ours with a child with a disability. Starting early with support staff and substitute caregivers can help ease the transition as your loved one's care needs increase. Even with options for in-home care, there may come a day when a different service option becomes necessary. Keeping honest and open communication flowing is essential for the most positive outcomes.

There are questions to ask when you are seeking outside home-based care services. You will want to know information about minimum hours or services, what training is provided to caregivers, background checks, and rates and terms of service. Are you locked into a long-term contract, or can you choose to end services when you want without added fees? Are there government programs you can access to assist with the fees associated with care?

Checking in to senior day programs where your loved one can go during the day can be a good idea and you can use it in combination with home-based care to improve care options. Having options is more likely when you begin your research before you are at the point of needing to access services. It keeps you from making rash decisions and leads to better outcomes for everyone involved. Start doing your research early to find the best providers in your area.

If your loved one is a senior, linking yourself with the local agency on aging is a significant help. They may be able to do the searching for you, so you have an extra hand and help in finding the best fit for help in your area. Rely on the programs and aid that is available to you so you can preserve your strength and energy.

Even with these services, there may be times when a different plan needs to occur. If you have promised your loved one that they will never have to leave their home, it adds a significant amount of stress to your plate. If you have no other options or their care becomes too much to manage, you will feel even more guilt and grief overall because you broke your promise. It can be more helpful to address these concerns before caregiving comes into play or at least early in the game.

Support for Caregivers and Care Recipients

Having an open and honest dialogue and sharing that you want to offer all the support possible expresses your priority for your loved ones to have the highest level of care that they need. It is essential to reassure them that you will keep track of their evolving needs and make decisions for the best outcomes for their health and well-being. Remind them that they are part of the journey and involve them as much as possible in the discussion while considering their level of capability. The key is keeping open communication, managing expectations, and making decisions together whenever possible.

How are you currently feeling most supported by others? Establishing and understanding your support systems puts the ball in your court. Taking the time to find which member of your team can do specific tasks is a terrific way to reduce your stress and overwhelm and allow those team members to be alongside you offering support. This may be a time to go back to your care team and decide whether the members still fit your current needs. It could be time to add a gerontologist, a dementia specialist, or a mental health professional. As you continue to build your support systems, recognize that you are just one person. There are only so many hats and roles one person can play.

At the minimum I was a mom, a wife, a daughter, an employee, and a caregiver. How many "ands" can one person handle? Keeping yourself in the game for the long run is the purpose of these strategies. The frantic nature of early caregiving eventually begins to ease, and you will have transitioned from a sprint to a marathon. Use your time and energy wisely so you and your loved ones have the best opportunity for health and well-being.

Preparing for the Changes and Adjustments of Caregiving

Long-term caregiving is a time to also take inventory of your living space. Is your home accessible, safe, and meeting the needs of the care recipient? Figure out whether modifications or adaptations are necessary at this stage of care. Creating an accessible home doesn't always mean major renovations. While installing ramps or grab bars can be essential, there are simpler, less involved fixes that can make a significant difference in improving accessibility for both the caregiver and care recipient. Switching to level-style door handles and faucet handles, rather than traditional knobs, can provide ease of use for someone with limited hand strength. Even adding brighter, more strategic lighting in hallways and stairways can prevent accidents. Another simple fix is placing commonly used items within reach, eliminating the need for frequent bending or stretching beyond a safe limit. You can also purchase specific, durable medical equipment to meet your needs. Many communities have donated equipment or equipment loans programs so you can trial items before making a purchase or to determine if a specific piece of equipment meets your needs. You may find your home is no longer the best solution and consider moving to a different living situation rather than retrofitting your current home. None of these are easy decisions but they are all things that are helpful to consider in the face of long-term caregiving.

If your loved one is moving in with you, it is helpful to have discussions about how the living arrangements will work. Is there a separate space for them in your home or will they be sharing the space you occupy? Is your home free of tripping hazards such as rugs, cords, and furniture? What about the necessity of using stairs? If they use adaptive equipment such as walkers or wheelchairs, are they easy to maneuver in the space as it is, or will you need to rearrange the environment? Are there funds available to make changes and modifications to the home? If you have other family members who will be sharing care maybe your loved one will travel from home to home. The scenarios can be as varied as the family or care partners can discover and discovery takes time.

Another big part of our lives is our employment situations. We gain a part of our identity from our position and our employment. When I realized I could no longer work as a speech-language pathologist, I felt incredible grief and loss. It was not just a job, it was an identity, and one I felt at my core.

It may be necessary to take a leave of absence or cut back on work hours in the face of long-term caregiving expectations. We discovered in our pandemic-era the options available for remote or hybrid work options. I attempted to work as a teletherapy speech-language pathologist both for the school district and for a private speech therapy company. Unfortunately, because of my brain injury, the demands of viewing a screen, the challenges of structuring and coordinating a schedule, and the fixed position of my body made this practice impossible for me to manage.

For many people, remote work is a wonderful option and can make a significant difference in their ability to maintain both their identity in their career and keep them financially stable. It is always an option to discuss work situations with an employer to see how you can continue to support your work and your family in a different way and still maintain the financial benefits of employment.

Remember your care recipient may be having these same feelings of loss. They have also lost a part of themselves and what they believed this part of their journey would look like. This is especially true when the need for care arises quickly and unexpectedly. Fear and apprehension about what the rest of their life may look like are normal emotions. Open communication and support are essential on both sides of the care continuum. These can be bonding moments as you learn and process the next steps on your journey together. You can still have positive outcomes with a different vision and a new set of experiences.

Planning for the Future

Another aspect of long-term caregiving is to know who is going to be involved. If you are caring for aging parents, who will be the primary caregiver? If you have siblings or other caregivers, is everyone going to be involved in the day-to-day care plans or is that impossible due to distances or strained family dynamics? It often falls to the family member who is closest in proximity to cover a significant amount of the care of a loved one. If something happens to the primary caregiver what is your backup plan?

Taking the time to have discussions about what caregiving might look like in best-case and worst-case scenarios is realistic and it is always better to be prepared. A care manager can ease these conversations. This is particularly helpful in situations where everyone is not on the same page. Having a third party involved at this point can significantly reduce tension.

Hope is not a strategy.

So often we have experiences where people "hope" they never need care. That is always a goal and a desire. I fully believe in hope and believe it is something we should never give up on. However, hope is not a strategy, so taking the time to be realistic, address the elephant in the room, and keep planning and moving forward is best for everyone involved. Planning is truly one of the best options you have in helping to make your caregiving as easy as possible. Even though the norm is waiting until something significant happens to begin to make decisions about caregiving, this is not ideal. It is likely you will need to have more than one conversation as you process through what long-term caregiving might look like for you.

Taking the opportunity to build in these conversations as a normal part of life is something to strive for. We spend more time planning and discussing events like birthdays, weddings, and one-time events than we ever do discussing issues that will have a significant impact in our lives. Having these discussions as a matter-of-fact conversation only normalizes this part of life. Whether we want to accept it or not we are all going to be involved in some level of care in our lifetimes.

I see people every day in my work in home health care who are woefully unprepared for caregiving. The time sneaks up on us and before we know it, we are one fall away from a significant life change. Planning ahead for the steps we are all going to encounter is not only smart, but also essential to having the most possible options in the future.

Continuing Mindfulness

If you have not already realized or prioritized the importance of supporting emotional health in caregiving, you will need it in the space of long-term caregiving. The longer you take on this role, the more essential emotional health becomes as the level of stress continues to be present. Long-term chronic stress affects your overall physical health and can lead to chronic illness for you as the caregiver.

Continuing to engage in the practices of mindfulness and self-care during caregiving can supply you with enough energy and resilience to get through the challenges. Know that you are not failing if you falter. Caregiving is a messy bundle at times and there is no shame in seeking help. In fact, you are doing yourself, your loved one, and your entire family a favor by getting the support you need in managing your challenging emotions. There is a direct correlation between caregiver well-being and the quality of care provided. So, caring for yourself, prioritizing your needs, and finding time to just be you aside from the title of caregiver is in everyone's best interests.

Keeping the lines of communication open in all directions is essential as the days turn to months and years of caring for one another.

Staying active in your community and engaging with other caregivers helps you to learn about added resources, keeps you feeling confident in your skills, and gives you the opportunity to pass your skills on to others. Isolation in caregiving is a very real issue and you deserve support to keep you functioning at your highest potential in caring. Attending educational events, accessing respite care, and finding the people you need to support you can make this space seem far less lonely and overwhelming.

Continue to expect change and evolving care plan needs. It may seem that as soon as you get something in place it changes. If you can understand and get comfortable with change it is just that much easier when it happens, because it will. Maintaining the ability to flex and flow in the care space is better for your overall well-being. By taking the time to practice the goal setting we discussed in Chapter 7, you can develop realistic and achievable goals for care.

Let yourself align with the caregiving journey and when your journey is complete, find satisfaction in terms of how you were able to influence the life of another. Pass that knowledge on and pay it forward. Caregivers all need and deserve the knowledge you develop. We must be there to support one another in this complicated realm. Our strength lies in community and the knowledge that we are not alone on our journey can be the thought that sustains us on the most difficult of days.

CHAPTER 8:
Chapter Questions and Workbook

Reflection Questions:

What have you grieved in your caregiving journey? Have you started having conversations with your family about aging and caregiving or end-of-life wishes? Have you connected with planners or advisers who may be helpful for your specific situation? How do you see yourself dealing with the stress of long-term caregiving?

Journal Prompts:

- Caregiving can be emotionally exhausting. Reflect on a recent moment when you felt overwhelmed and drained. How did you cope at that moment? What can you do to build emotional resilience for future challenges?

_____

_____

_____

_____

- What are your current family dynamics related to caregiving? How are you feeling about care planning and sharing responsibilities?

- What planning, discussions, and resources do you need to have in place to prepare for future caregiving needs?

Action Steps:

Supporting your emotional health is crucial in long-term caregiving. Changes can happen quickly and often. Take the opportunity to develop your skills in mindfulness through guided meditations and visualization. Use your senses to find a space of relaxation within your day-to-day caring. Below is one example of mindfulness you can use. Find what works best for you and continue to practice so you can have peace of mind in challenging times.

Listen to the Audio:
Melody shares a Guided Meditation:

http://www.melodyvachal.com/audio-resources

Visualize yourself in a relaxing setting. Maybe it is on a beach or in nature or you are in a special place inside your mind. Your body is still and quiet and you are feeling rested. What are the words or thoughts you are speaking internally? Are they kind, loving, and compassionate? Is your mind resting or are the thoughts still flowing quickly? Let them slow and find a pause in your busy mind. Notice whether you hear any sound. You don't need to pay attention to it. Just notice the sound and let it go. Is the sun coming up or setting? Can you feel a breeze or is there warmth in the air? Maybe you have a cup of coffee or a favorite beverage you are sipping? Can you smell the aroma? As you take a sip, notice the flavor, and savor the moment. Let all your senses notice the space you are in and just be in the moment. No action is needed. You can just pause and breathe deeply for this moment. It is available for you when you need it. Peace is within you if you allow it to be.

"Our greatest glory is not in never failing, but in rising every time we fail."
— Ralph Waldo Emerson

CHAPTER 9:
Facing Challenges and Setbacks

No one ever said life was supposed to be easy and nowhere does that seem truer than in caregiving. The day-to-day commitment and intensity can overshadow your life in a way you could not have imagined before you took on this role. From personal experience, I know that it is not an easy experience from either side of the equation – caregiver or care recipient. I have lived both and they each come with their own inherent challenges.

One day that illustrated the nature of setbacks comes immediately to mind. It was a beautiful, sunny day in the summer of 1996. Isaac was 6 months old, and his health had stabilized. I decided it would be an enjoyable day to attend an arts fair in our community. I packed up his stroller and supplies and we headed over to the fair. I wandered aimlessly from booth to booth, visiting with the vendors and even ran into a few friends. Isaac was sleeping peacefully in the stroller, and I sat on a grassy hill with the warm sun on my back and a glass of ice-cold lemonade. He started to wake up and when he did, instead of stretching, his little head jerked forward quickly, and his arms pulled into his chest. I had noticed this once or twice before he was fully awake, but I assumed his nervous system was acclimating after all the trauma he had been through. The next time it happened, it did not stop at once or twice, the pattern continued repeatedly maybe twenty times before it stopped.

I had a sick feeling in my stomach as I knew this was not normal, so I quickly pushed his stroller away from the crowds and I made a call to the clinic. The pediatrician I spoke with was concerned and wanted to see him, so we left and went to the clinic. She believed from my description that he was having a type of seizure called infantile spasms and quickly made an appointment for us to travel back to the Children's Hospital in the next few days for further testing and neurological evaluation. I was terrified while taking him home that something life-threatening was going to happen again and was grateful when we made it to the appointment a few days later.

They admitted Isaac to the hospital for tests and after completing EEGs and evaluations, the diagnosis of infantile spasms was confirmed. Isaac had seizures after his first admission to the hospital at 10 weeks old but had not had any since returning home, so this was devastating. The neurologist told us three potential outcomes were possible: Isaac's seizures would go away, the seizures would stay the same as they were, or they would progress, and with that progression would come progressive delays and a loss of abilities. I just could not believe everything that had already happened; we were back into the mode of trauma once again.

At the Children's Hospital, they felt the best course of action was to begin treating him with a drug called ACTH, adrenocorticotropic hormone – a steroid that needed to be given as an injection. I stayed at the hospital with Isaac as I needed to learn another new skill, which was how to inject Isaac with the ACTH. This was not a skill I relished or wanted to learn but again I had no choice. Isaac needed this medication so I practiced on my orange and tried to get better at the jabbing motion I would need to be able to pierce his soft baby skin. It seemed so unfair that he should have to go through this every day. When I returned home, a public health nurse came out for the first day or two to make sure I did the injection correctly and then it was my ongoing duty. As hard as it was to do, the hardest part was when he no longer cried with the injection. He was simply used to the experience, which quite honestly broke my heart.

As time passed, the seizures stopped but the effects of the medication caused extreme changes in Isaac. He was extremely irritable, had significant weight gain, acquired a "moon face" appearance, and his health had to be watched very closely. It brought with it potential high-risk issues such as hypertension, hyperglycemia, and gastrointestinal bleeding. It also suppressed his immune system, so we had to be incredibly careful about interacting with others. If there were any signs of even a minor illness, the doctor needed to be notified at once. The hypervigilance needed to care for him 24 hours a day was exhausting. Hours were spent with him in the baby swing, and he would cry and bang the side of his face. His little face was so swollen his eyes were just slits.

There were days when I honestly thought I would lose my mind but there was no choice but to do this for Isaac. It was the best treatment option we had available to us and even with all the side effects, it was working, and the seizures were stopping. As Isaac began to wean off the medication, he started to lose the effects of the steroid. He began to return to his normal size and shape and the extreme irritability was decreasing. Once again, I was hopeful this would be a fresh start, and we could find a place of rest and pause. Six months passed and all was still going well. My guard had dropped slightly although, there was always a hyperfocus on any slight change or difference in his condition.

It was January and Brenna and her dad were off on an adventure. They had taken the opportunity to go ice fishing with friends. It is true - ice fishing is a real thing in Minnesota. You sleep in a fish house on a frozen lake, and it is a combination of winter camping and sporting activities. I was a little reluctant to let them go because I am a worrier, but they were very excited, and off they went. It was January 4, 1997 – what would have been my daughter R.C.'s second birthday – when Isaac's seizures returned. Of all the 365 days in a year it had to happen today? I was devastated and could not bear to think where this would lead. It seemed no matter which way I turned there was always a crisis. About the time I would get my bearings from the last upheaval, another club would come along and hit me upside the head. Our daily life seemed to consist of treading lightly in hopes that the next awful thing would not happen or that there would be a longer pause before it did.

Understanding Your Uniqueness and Value as a Caregiver

Living with apprehension, chronic levels of stress, and hypervigilance takes its toll on individuals, couples, and families. This is the space where caregivers live each day. It comes as no surprise that marriages in families of children with special needs have staggering divorce statistics. The trauma we often see and live with as caregivers is not an easy companion and it is yet another reason that we must acknowledge the burdens and challenges that come with the role of caregiver. Understanding the significance of the journey allows you to consider why you may be struggling.

It makes sense why you feel overwhelmed, angry, and have significant emotional responses to caregiving. It can feel like walking on eggshells or a tightrope a good percentage of the time. Realizing all the extra stress that comes with caregiving is essential for you to understand the importance of what we have covered thus far. You must take the opportunity to lean on others and find support in whatever way makes sense to you and fits your current lifestyle. It takes courage to be vulnerable and allow others to help you, support you, and walk the journey alongside you.

You are an essential element in the care space and the responsibility is not one to take lightly. The fact is many people cannot do what you are doing or will be doing. The journey of caregiving is not one that everyone is willing to take, so give yourself credit for stepping up and embracing this important role. You are part of a unique group – those who step outside of themselves to care for others. Not everyone says yes when a need is present. Not everyone is capable or able to wear this important title of caregiver. You are unique, valued, and make a difference every single day. Do not ever believe what you are doing is not important, valuable, and necessary work.

Allowing Yourself to Ask for and Accept Help

One of my biggest challenges as a caregiver was acknowledging or even realizing that I needed help or could ask for it. Even when people offered, I was quick to brush it off. It was easier – or so I thought – to keep doing what I was doing because at least it was familiar. There was less fear in the familiar. I had systems in place and I knew what my role was. In fact, I relished my role because it made me feel secure. Even though it was difficult, I understood it. The routines and patterns allowed me to feel a sense of control and comfort in a space that often felt out of control.

What I did not know was why it was so necessary for me to share the load. I did not realize the depth of caregiving over the years ahead and, had I asked for help earlier or allowed others to support me, it would have been better for my mental and physical health, my relationships, and my overall quality of life. I held myself to a standard that was quite impossible to reach. I held so much fear, and a mind enveloped in fear does not allow peace and pause and self-compassion. It holds self-judgment, rigidity, and isolation. It was not something I talked about or even knew for a long time, but it was there. It was there in the control I held. It was there in the inability to let others take part in care. It was there in how I felt when I did not have support – which was often my own fault.

When people try to offer help and take part in your journey and you continually ignore their attempts, you lose opportunities. When you do not ask for input from a partner or spouse, you lose connection. When you seem to be a one-woman show, you lose community. I can look back now with a clearer vision and see that these are all losses that could have looked different. In any situation, you are only one person, and it is difficult to work in a void or a vacuum. You will find support if you allow it and seek it.

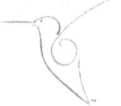

Allowing yourself to widen your lens to see the broader view and perspective can make all the difference in the world.

As a caregiver, you get myopic, and your tunnel vision does not allow you to see beyond the present moment. You cannot even imagine stepping outside of the day-to-day and believing there is more beyond this part of your life. It is difficult to realize that caregiving is not your whole life because it certainly can feel that way, especially on the hard days. We will all deal with caregiving in different and unique ways and problem-solve in ways that make sense to us. For me, that was control and fear for an exceedingly long time.

When I was helping to care for my father in his later years, I found myself in a situation where I had no choice but to reach out. It was the summer of 2009, and my dad had been in a transitional care unit receiving therapy and recovering from health problems. He had been there for a significant amount of time, and I would visit nearly every day and – between that and caring for Isaac – it had been a long summer. Thankfully, my dad was able to be discharged and return to his apartment. What a relief and joy it was to know he was going to get back to his normal routine and, after a great deal of demanding work on his part, he would be out of rehab. I felt like we had achieved a great win and was excited for him to return home.

He had only been home a brief time when he had a fall. For some reason, this time, it proved too much for me. I completely fell apart. I could not stop crying and I was distraught, at my final limits – it pushed me to the brink. I was still married at the time and my husband stayed alongside me, supported me, and encouraged me to reach out to my siblings. They, of course, were more than willing to manage aspects of the next steps, from researching and planning to jumping in for day-to-day activities. They had been part of the journey before but really launched into action when I was falling apart.

I finally sought out care from my doctor and I decided to try anxiety medication, which over time allowed me to feel more settled and I could see the way to a new perspective. This was the time when I realized I was not an island. Before that moment, I don't believe I ever realized I could ask others for help instead of continuing to take on more responsibilities, as I had always done before. I was my own worst enemy on that front and this situation clearly brought it to the forefront. I remain incredibly grateful for my family's support, and I wish I had realized sooner the impact of reaching out to allow others to care for me as well as the importance of seeking out medical and mental health professionals before things reach a point of critical mass.

Forging Ahead

I wish I could say the turning point lasted, and I was completely able to rely on others from that point forward, but memories fade quickly, and old patterns re-establish. Fast forward to 2016 and my accident, which started my true journey to the space of healing not only my broken body and broken brain, but my overall sense of who I was in the world and what my journey could mean to others. I was out of work for nine months following my accident, and when I first returned to my job, I was understandably apprehensive. I knew the difficulty my brain injury was causing me in being able to tolerate noise and lights, manage my emotions, and follow the flow of conversations.

I have a friend, Merith, who is also a speech-language pathologist, and, before the accident, we could execute multiple conversations and topics simultaneously with zero effort. There was a program called Strive for Five which was related to the number of conversational turns you would try to achieve with a child to develop interaction and communication skills. We would jokingly call our interactions "Yen for Ten." It always felt like we had our own full song and dance show, and during my career, I would jokingly say I was a rock star when others asked what I did for a living. Heading into an early childhood classroom was a delight, and I never knew exactly what to expect, but the children – or tiny humans as I liked to refer to them – would be so excited to see me. They would delight and erupt in excitement when I arrived and had so much wonder about what special activity or toy we might engage in each day. How could I manage or live up to the old days before the accident when I could barely even tolerate sound?

The first day back at work, my assignment was to sit in the classroom at the teacher's desk and not interact with the children. I was told to be there for 45 minutes and then I could leave. I came into this space where I had always thrived and within 20 minutes, I could not tolerate it anymore. The noise and the constant activity of the children was simply too much for me to bear. I left early and was physically ill when I arrived home. Twenty minutes?! This was the length of time one speech therapy session would typically last with my preschool students. How could I be effective or able to see the 15 to 20 students a day across multiple settings and travel in between sites as I had done for decades? Was this ever going to be a possibility again?

I felt utterly defeated and yet I had no choice but to try and forge ahead. My livelihood and my passion for my profession were at stake. This was only the beginning of my trials at returning to my pre-accident self in the work setting. For the next three years I tried a variety of options from a reduced work schedule to teletherapy – which was a complete failure as I felt stuck in a tiny room where it was impossible to leave the computer. This was also difficult for me as my brain injury and eye issues caused serious headaches. Dealing with all the physical and emotional aspects of the accident proved to be a struggle that was far greater than I had ever imagined.

In this situation, I was incredibly grateful to have Mary, a qualified rehabilitation consultant who worked as a liaison between me and the school system. She was an incredible advocate and made sure I had the support in place and was a true partner for four years, at which point the reality became clear to me that I would need to seek a new career. I took a leave of absence for my final year to reach retirement and transitioned into working with my former spouse in the business he built decades before to provide in-home care for Isaac. We needed care for him and could not find a company that delivered what we needed, so Jay founded Arise Cares. The need in our community was great and other families sought us out as they looked for care needs for their family members.

The company we now own together has continued to expand and currently serves seniors aging in place as well as children and families. This is another example of how, when facing obstacles, you can think creatively. This is exactly what happened – we needed care for Isaac, as the care we found was not meeting our expectations. The result of thinking creatively allowed us not only to find the care Isaac needed but also to provide care for so many others in the same boat. What a blessing it is to be able to support families like ours. I am grateful for the insight and determination Jay showed in founding a business that kept Isaac well cared for and supported and continues to offer this same gift to others.

You do not need to start a company to show resilience. Instead, it is about what you can do when challenges present themselves, as they will in caregiving. Prioritizing yourself and practicing self-care is a necessity and a gift of resilience and self-compassion. Your success comes in small ways, such as maintaining social connections with others so you can feel supported. Deciding to join a support group or hire a coach so you can build the resilience you need to stay motivated and move forward in seeking the best outcomes for your life journey. You have the choice to grow beyond your challenges and not to be defined by them.

Expecting Change and Facing Challenges

As a caregiver, the only constant is change. There are any number of challenges, crises, and disappointments along the way: illnesses, treatments that may or not be helpful, split-second decisions in medical emergencies, and even the loss of care staff or secondary caregivers who do not fulfill their roles, as well as many other issues. Physical and emotional stress are a daily part of the caregiving experience. Caring for someone, especially long-term, can be physically and emotionally draining. Caregivers often experience fatigue, burnout, anxiety, and depression. Social isolation is a common experience as a caregiver.

The demands of caregiving can make it difficult to keep a social life and connections with friends and family outside of the caregiving situation. Financial strain can be a significant challenge which adds to the stress on a family and relationships. Caregiving costs like medical bills, supplies, and home modifications can put a significant financial burden on caregivers and their families. Knowing where to turn to find the needed resources and services can feel like a full-time job. It is no surprise that caregivers often feel unprepared or lack the proper training to oversee complex medical tasks or challenging behaviors. We all enter the caregiving space with different talents and temperaments. If you are out of alignment with others in the care space, it can be difficult to discover how you will manage the responsibilities.

Balancing work and caregiving when things are stable is challenging enough and if you add in anything extra (like a life-altering accident) I can tell you the stress is more than one can handle without significant support and encouragement from others. Trying to juggle a career with caregiving responsibilities can be extremely difficult and stressful. There is a reason many people must leave their places of employment when caregiving responsibilities surface. Disagreements over care decisions, expectations, and boundaries can cause tension and strife within families. Situations where you watch a loved one's health deteriorate over time can be heartbreaking for caregivers. There will never be a shortage of setbacks or adversity in caring.

As a person receiving care, challenges also abound. You are dealing with the loss of your sense of self and how you show up in the world.

No one expects to be in a situation in which you are now dependent on another person to help you meet even the most basic needs. I had always been able to manage my life and responsibilities without a second thought. To be at a point where I had to ask for assistance and wait for help from others caused me to feel less than, to feel like I was a burden, a problem, and not as valuable as I was before the accident. I lost a sense of who I was and what I would be good for if I were not caring for others. Did I have inherent value as only Melody? Was I worthy if I were just me as an individual? Did I matter if I was not the caregiver, and I was now in need of care?

There are endless questions and difficulties in being the person in need of care and I was completely unprepared to be on the receiving end of it. This is something we all need to think about because the likelihood is that we are highly likely to need care from another at some point in our lives. The preparation could be as simple as beginning to have conversations about how I might feel if I needed significant help from another person in my daily life. How would I like that to look? What would I like if I could choose? How do I want to define and design my life going forward?

We are all on a journey through life and as we age our needs change. It is wise to have open and compassionate conversations about potential future care requirements. While discussing this topic can feel uncomfortable, avoiding it will not make those possibilities go away. Approaching it with empathy, both for ourselves and our loved ones, can help us plan thoughtfully. Preparing to maintain our abilities for as long as possible and preparing for different scenarios allows us to face the future with dignity, no matter what lies ahead.

Setting yourself up for success and developing resiliency to overcome challenging situations can be done in any number of ways. Realize that you are on your own journey, and it may look different than what you imagined. A different life than expected can still be a worthwhile and fulfilling experience. We each have one life to live, and your only limits are your own thoughts and dreams. Gratitude for the steps in your journey can help you shift your focus from disappointment to acceptance and contentment if you allow it to do so.

It is normal and healthy to grieve loss and process a new reality. Take the time to process when challenges and disappointments come your way. Step forward in whatever tiny steps you can and eventually those tiny steps will create milestones and new possibilities. The pain may always be there, and you still have the strength within to keep going. Even tiny steps are steps and progress toward acceptance and fulfillment in a life that is different than you imagined. Do not let the quest or belief in perfection keep you from moving on and attaining your best life. Even though the destination may be unexpected, find joy in the journey. You deserve it.

CHAPTER 9:
Chapter Questions and Workbook

Reflection Questions:

What challenges have you experienced on your caregiving journey? What did you learn about yourself through the challenges you have faced? How are you finding support in demanding situations? Who are your supporters?

Journal Prompts:

- Think about a recent setback or disappointment you experienced on your caregiving journey. How did it make you feel? What were your reactions to the situation? What things did you learn about yourself through the setback and how can they help you in the future?

_____

_____

_____

_____

- How do you communicate with others when you are feeling overwhelmed? What are strategies you can use to ask for support from others?

_____

_____

_____

_____

_____

Action Steps:

Imagine that you are encouraging a friend who is going through a challenging time. Write a letter to him or her offering support and uplifting them on their journey. When you finish, read it to yourself and try to remember all the ways you can offer yourself compassion just as you do for others.

"Character cannot be developed in ease and quiet. Only through experience of trial and suffering can the soul be strengthened, ambition inspired, and success achieved." — Helen Keller

CHAPTER 10:
The Road Ahead

Do you remember those glorious days of childhood when you had no responsibilities and no worries, and the days flowed like slow-moving clouds across the sky? From my childhood days growing up on the North Dakota prairie, I could not have imagined all the twists and turns my life has held. The charm of my small-town childhood is hard to describe to someone who has not experienced it. There was freedom in leaving my home on the farm where I lived with my parents and five older brothers and sisters and riding my bike a mile into our small hometown. I would spend summer days getting up early and working in the garden before I biked into town to hang out with my friends. Friday nights brought open stores and a bandstand with a musical program or a watermelon giveaway.

As the youngest, I had the benefit of the experiences of my siblings. When I arrived, my parents had their skill set dialed in and I had a carefree childhood. I learned about community and care from my parents and what I witnessed in my hometown. People knew you, your grandparents, aunts, and uncles. When challenges arrived, the community pulled together. You knew if your neighbors were struggling, and everyone banded together with cooperation and compassion.

I have deep gratitude for such an idyllic childhood. From the earliest memories of my life, I had a sense of connection to both my family and my community. I was able to watch my mother care for friends and neighbors. We would deliver meals on wheels to those in need and if someone were ill or had a crisis you did not give a thought to lending a hand. It was just what you did.

I never realized how much this sense of community and support would shape not only my childhood but also the remainder of my life. I learned that life was not just about me as an individual. It was about community and making sure others were supported and cared for. Was I always a caregiver? In some ways, I was. Not in the way I am a caregiver now, but learning to be in community with others was the first step in the journey of supporting and wanting more for the greater good. It shaped my life and helped me understand that we all need one another while we walk this earth together.

We need to understand that what impacts us individually flows to our communities and on a larger scale has a global impact. Nowhere is this clearer than in the space of raising awareness and consciousness on the topic of caregiving, the impact on the individuals who provide care, and how caregiving is impacting our world as the caregiving crisis continues.

The Financial and Physical Effects of Caregiving

There are 55 million caregivers in the United States who are providing unpaid care to family members. On top of the employment caregivers may already hold, they are coming home to another full-time job – one with no pay or financial benefits. Not to mention the additional impacts caregiving has on their "real" jobs. Caregivers may have to reduce their work hours, take unpaid leave, or quit their jobs entirely to provide care. This loss of income in the short term causes additional stress in an already high-stress situation.

In the long term, the loss of income and career opportunities may have lifelong effects. Caregivers, many of them women, may already be paid less than their male counterparts due to unequal pay for equal work. This income is often lost during the years of highest earning potential and can thus change lifetime earning potential. The loss of income and potential promotions impacts retirement outcomes and planning for the future in terms of retirement and financial security overall.

Additionally, caregivers may have to dip into their savings or retirement funds to cover expenses. There are often significant out-of-pocket expenses for medical equipment, home modifications, additional caregiving support, and other caregiving-related expenses. The physical and emotional toll of caregiving can lead to higher healthcare costs for the caregivers themselves. We know caregivers experience higher rates of chronic illness due to increased stress, depression, and other health issues.

There is also the fact that caregivers frequently neglect their own healthcare needs when caring for another person and it is not unusual for a care provider to die sooner than their care recipient. Health issues that may have been diagnosed early do not surface until an illness is much worse or even life-threatening. Informal and family caregivers often have minimal if any training in proper techniques for things like lifting, medication management, or bathing. There is a greater risk of physical injury due to the demands of caregiving which can then cycle back into absenteeism and employment issues.

Whether caring for children, attending to the needs of an aging family member, or caring for someone ill, workplaces need to support employees and understand the demands of caregiving.

The Need for Employer Support

Many family caregivers are not able to afford outside care to support their loved ones. Even when they can, such in-home or assisted living care workers are often poorly paid and there is a significantly high turnover rate. If you are fortunate and able to pay for care, it is still an added expense the average family is not facing. This is precisely why we need to continue to support caregivers in the workforce. We need the employees to continue to work to run our businesses and generate economic growth and tax revenues to provide the necessary programs to support these same family caregivers. If employers were more aware of the family caregivers among their staff, they would benefit from offering support in the workplace to help these employees maintain their jobs and better understand the roles they take on outside of work.

The sheer volume of family caregivers additionally holding down jobs is often unknown by employers. Employees are often reluctant to identify themselves as caregivers. They may be concerned that, if their situation is out in the open, they will become a target under the watchful eye of employers or fellow employees. They may worry about facing discrimination or stereotypes related to their ability to balance work commitments on top of their caregiving responsibilities. Caregivers worry that they may seem less professional or less resolute due to the extra work they perform as caregivers. This can impact their career advancement.

If the workplace does not have policies to support caregiving employees, there can be a level of fear and vulnerability in identifying their situation. How can employers be supportive of these employees? Exploring the options of flexible scheduling and accommodations for the unique demands of the caregiver adds to employee satisfaction.

One way to accomplish this is by establishing flexible work options. This flexibility could be accomplished through a hybrid model, where an employee can work from home, have flexible hours, or compress their work week. Having the freedom to set their schedule allows caregivers to manage their caregiving responsibilities while continuing to excel in their jobs. Job sharing may be another option for a family caregiver if full-time employment is not possible in the short term but there is still a need for a salary to continue supporting the current family care needs.

Taking the time to search out community resources such as elder care services and support or childcare networks can also be a way to show your employees that you have their best interests at heart.

Familiarizing yourself with services available locally and partnering with other businesses to best serve your staff is a practical way to support your employees while building your network and setting yourself apart from other employers. Policies like paid family leave, respite care, and other support services such as caregiver coaching and employee assistance programs not only help you to hold on to current employees but also attract new employees to your business. Employees have more options these days and are no longer willing to "die at their desks" to the detriment of their health and the needs of their families.

Having open conversations about caregiving and the responsibilities that accompany it is another crucial step in establishing a culture that cares. The ability to share authentically with coworkers and management creates support and encourages the sharing of common experiences. This can ward off those feelings of isolation which are common for caregivers. The more comfortable an employee feels, the more likely he or she is to stay committed to an employer.

Striving to create an atmosphere that demonstrates the value of work-life balance is crucial. Managers and owners play a pivotal role by practicing work-life balance in their own lives and respecting their employees' boundaries. Management staff should have training and be equipped with skills to recognize signs of stress and burnout and help employees with extraordinary circumstances. A mutual level of respect allows employees to feel comfortable if they need extra help or time off for caregiving responsibilities.

Highlighting employee assistance programs, hiring coaches, and prioritizing the emotional and mental well-being of employees all represent a great step in the right direction. Accessing wellness workshops and programs specific to caregiver employees can promote overall well-being. These resources show that the company cares about its employees' health and happiness. When companies are striving to support work-life balance, it makes for happier and more productive employees. The demands of caregiving frequently impact social connections and being able to continue to work and maintain relationships with colleagues can decrease the sense of isolation that often accompanies care.

Good employees can be hard to come by, and one of caregiver employees' great strengths is balancing multiple responsibilities. Employee retention, satisfaction, and commitment to the job are just a few of the bonuses that accompany support. By prioritizing your commitment to these workers and creating an environment where work and caregiving can coexist, companies can foster a culture of inclusivity and support.

The Impact of Caregiving on the Healthcare System

While employment issues for caregivers are important, it is equally important to recognize the profound impact of caregiving on supporting the healthcare system by allowing family members to remain in their homes as long as possible. Society benefits on the backs of family caregivers as they continue to provide the bulk of long-term care in the United States. The healthcare system saves billions of dollars each year thanks to the daily sacrifices made by family caregivers. This challenging work, though rooted in compassion for family, is often overlooked and goes unnoticed in our society.

Care recipients' ability to age in place and remain in the comfort of their own homes or the homes of their caregivers decreases the burden on institutions that are already having difficulty accessing paid caregivers. At some point in life, most people will either need a family caregiver or be one. In my case both were true. This became evident during the coronavirus pandemic when family caregivers acted as frontline care for their loved ones. Whether you are a youth caregiver or caring for children, young adults, or older relatives or friends, the likelihood of supporting and supplementing healthcare systems through unpaid family caregiving is likely to continue and expand as the population continues to age.

Long-term services and support provided by family caregivers help reduce financial burdens for those in need of care, which in turn eases the strain on systems like Medicaid. Without such support, Medicaid spending can quickly surpass other state priorities, including education and economic development. As a society, we must become aware of and support the needs of family caregivers to shoulder the burden of care by continuing to build capacity in the skills and training of family caregivers.

We must advocate for comprehensive support, including financial assistance and employment benefits like family medical leave and flexible work arrangements. Additionally, it's crucial that healthcare systems integrate family caregiving into the care continuum and care planning to enhance the outcomes for those in need of care.

The Need for Support in Underserved and Rural Communities

We must also work to provide additional support for those living in rural or underserved areas. Documented barriers to the access to services include lack of service options, poor transportation options, low internet connectivity, poor access to training and education, shortages of healthcare workers, social isolation, cultural competency, and economic disadvantages. As someone who grew up in a rural area, I understand the challenges that accompany rural caregiving.

Access to home health services, hospice, adult day programs, and transportation are significant needs impacting rural caregiving. It is not unusual to travel great distances for care and there is a significant healthcare workforce shortage. This lack of support places an even greater burden on a family caregiver. Internet connectivity issues can limit access to training, education, and online support.

Social isolation is a common issue for caregivers, and in underserved and rural communities, the lack of transportation options severely limits a caregiver's ability to step away and take breaks from their caregiving responsibilities. Higher poverty rates are evident in these areas too, which can make having substitute or secondary caregivers near impossible. In underserved minority communities, language barriers and cultural stigmas may impact the ability to access care and help for caregivers. Culturally competent training and providers may also be lacking, which continues to promote isolation and reduces the ability to connect with others in similar circumstances.

We must seek to build our home- and community-based services in these areas by accessing and increasing funding to provide development of the long-term services and support for caregivers. Investments in technology and transportation as well as developing a robust rural healthcare system are crucial to support family caregivers now and into the future.

Continuing Self-care, Team Building, and Communication

As we wrap up this journey through caregiving, it is important to remember that caring for others begins with caring for yourself. Self-care is not a luxury; it is a necessity. It is a responsibility to yourself. The physical and emotional demands of caregiving can be overwhelming and, without proper attention to your own needs, burnout can take a heavy toll. Prioritize moments of rest, relaxation, and personal joy. By recharging yourself, you will be able to offer the best care to those who depend on you. Every day do at least one thing just for yourself. A cup of tea, a chat with a friend, or even a long deep breath are simple and effective ways to prioritize your own well-being.

Caregiving is not a solo endeavor. Building your care team is vital to ensuring that you have the resources to support yourself. Relying on friends and family along with professionals can help you attain the support that you and those you care for need. Setting up routines and systems to make your days flow more easily is essential for successful caregiving. Allow others to join you. I wish I had realized that earlier on in my own caregiving journey. It can feel frightening and vulnerable to ask for help. Be brave in your attempts. You will not regret it.

Setting goals for yourself and including your care recipient in the process will build strength in your relationship and decrease your feeling of being alone in the trenches. Even small steps are progress and being able to measure your progress through small objectives and goals helps keep things moving. There will be challenges and setbacks along the way. They are part of everyone's life and do not define you. Being adaptable in the face of challenges will help you to move forward even when the path is difficult. Setbacks are simply opportunities to gain experience. They teach us patience and perseverance. Each obstacle you overcome gives you the strength to continue.

Advocacy is another key aspect of caregiving. It can feel uncomfortable at times but remember you are not just a caregiver. You are the voice of the one you care for and making sure they receive the best possible care requires you to speak up for them. This means developing new skills, navigating complex systems, and being creative in your problem-solving. Remember to celebrate the victories and milestones you achieve along the way. Everyone's journey has a different number of steps and realizing you are making progress provides you with the motivation and hope you need to keep going. Reflect on your growth and give yourself those pats on the back for all you have achieved and the differences you are making in the life of another.

Caregiving is not just a physical responsibility; it is an emotional and psychological journey that can deeply affect every part of you. The constant balancing act between caregiving and your own life can stir feelings of guilt, shame, frustration, and even resentment. Let yourself acknowledge these emotions without judgment. Caregiving, while rewarding, is hard. It is normal to feel overwhelmed at times. The key is to remember that your emotions do not define you or overshadow the love and dedication you bring to this journey.

The emotional toll of caregiving and your experiences, both challenging and celebratory, open the door to incredible personal growth. You can find inner strength, patience, and resilience you would have never imagined. Allow yourself to grieve the losses you experience as you also celebrate the connection and depths of compassion that caregiving brings to your life. You will be changed forever by your experiences of caregiving. At times it may be more than you can manage alone. Seek professional help or support groups if needed. Just as you advocate for your loved one you must also advocate for your own emotional and mental well-being. Taking care of yourself keeps you strong on this windy caregiving road.

To close this chapter, let this be your call to action. I encourage you to share your journey with others. Be honest about your challenges, struggles, and growth. Let others benefit from your knowledge and experiences. Your life story may be just the thing someone else needs to hear so they can keep going. When you share your experiences with honesty, you empower others and help them to feel less alone on their journey. This support network will continue to grow and develop so that we can pave the way for the next generation of caregivers. Together we can continue to strengthen those who care for others and lift them up to do the same. The journey you are on is challenging and rewarding. It requires strength, compassion, and resilience. The work you do matters. You matter. You are valuable. May you be strong. May you be compassionate. May you find joy in your journey and always remember to take care of you!

CHAPTER 10:
Chapter Questions and Workbook

Reflection Questions:

Have you shared your journey with another caregiver? What similarities and differences do you notice between you and others who are caregivers? What have been your greatest challenges and your greatest successes at this point of your journey? How can you support others in this journey?

Journal Prompts:

- What are your greatest hopes and concerns for the road ahead of you as a caregiver? What might you do to plan for both unknown challenges and the unexpected?

_____

_____

_____

_____

_____

- How has caregiving influenced your ability to find a balance between personal time, family time, caregiving, and work? What strategies have helped you and what can you improve on going forward?

- What would you have told yourself at the start of your journey that would make it easier for you to feel supported and successful?

- Take the opportunity to retake the stress assessment. Rate yourself from 1 meaning never and 10 meaning always. What, if any, changes are you seeing from your initial assessment in Chapter 1? What might you do differently as you move forward based on what you read in this book?

Post-Test

Question	Rating (1-10)	Notes
How often do you feel overwhelmed by caregiving?		
How are you balancing your caregiving duties with other aspects of your life (e.g. work, personal time)?		
How often do you find yourself physically exhausted due to caregiving?		
How often do you find time for yourself for self-care or activities that help you relax?		
How frequently do you experience feelings of guilt related to caregiving?		
How often do you feel emotionally drained by caregiving?		
How well do you think you manage stress when unexpected caregiving challenges occur?		
How frequently do you experience loneliness or isolation as a caregiver?		
How supported do you feel (by friends, family, community resources) in your caregiving role?		
How confident are you in your ability to continue in your caregiving role without significantly impacting your own health?		

Action Steps

Identify two or three immediate goals and the next steps you will take based on what you have learned from the book. Reflect on your progress and share your journey with others. Use what you have learned to maintain balance in your life and empower yourself and others in the essential role of caregiving.

As we close, remember that your journey as a caregiver holds immense value – not only for you and your care recipient but also for the wider caregiving community. By sharing your experiences, insights, and challenges, you offer a guiding light to others walking a similar path. Together we can lift one another up, drawing strength from our shared experiences and working together in community for the greater good. Together may we find resilience, hope, and the power to make a lasting difference. Keep rising – your voice matters.

**Watch Video:
Melody Shares a Personal Message:**

https://www.melodyvachal.com/personal-message

Acknowledgements

When life leads you on a path that is unexpected and filled with challenges, you have a choice. You can succumb or you can rise to meet the challenge at hand. This book has been a labor of love for me and a call to action for those who live in caregiving spaces. It is not an easy journey, and every day provides you with new opportunities for growth. As caregivers, we often navigate a world we do not understand and are fearful of entering. We continue to chart the course, hoping and praying for still water and a successful voyage. My voyage has not always been smooth sailing, but I am still afloat.

I would like to acknowledge those who have supported and encouraged me on this journey. First, I acknowledge my parents George and Jean Olson. Although they are no longer with me on this earth, they are still in my heart and soul. They laid the groundwork and provided me with a heart of service and a legacy of hard work and determination that has served me well for all the twists and turns I have encountered.

To my children, thank you for teaching me how to love unconditionally and bringing abundant joy into my life. You inspire me to heal, persevere, and keep going even on the hardest days. To Brenna, you delight me with your outlook, intelligence, and passion. I have learned much from you about letting go and letting God carry the burdens. You are not just my daughter but my dear friend. To R.C., my angel baby. Thank you for making the journey to this world so I could hold you even for the briefest time. I am eternally grateful. To Isaac, for being pure love and teaching me to find joy in the simple things. You continue to be one of my greatest teachers. To Shane, you have filled my life with beautiful music, and I marvel at your gifts and talents. Your gentle heart and spirit and love of family are inspiring. You all remind me to be brave and face challenges head on and for that I am grateful. This book is for you all as much as it is for the world. May it remind you of the strength and courage you hold within.

To my partner, JJ, thank you for your encouragement, your unwavering support, and your belief in me and this project. You never doubted I could do it and you kept me moving forward with light, love, and laughter. You are the icing on the cake, and I love you.

I extend my heartfelt appreciation to all the therapists, medical professionals, and educators who have been part of our journey. Your knowledge, compassion, and dedication have not only helped me heal and recover but also navigate and grow as an advocate for Isaac and myself.

A special thanks to my editorial and production team, Mattie Murrey and Tamara Monosoff. You believed in me and my story and collaborated with me to bring this project to life. Your guidance and support helped me share my experiences and ideas and author my story in a way that I hope will touch the lives of many.

To my incredible beta readers, whose insights and feedback shaped this book into what it is today: your dedication and honesty were invaluable. Your perspectives helped ensure that this guide speaks to the hearts of those walking this challenging path.

To my sister, Cheryl, thank you for your ability in identifying editorial changes and helping to create a bio and back cover that define my unique experiences. I am so grateful for your love and support.

To my brother, Brad, thank you for shooting my author photo and capturing my essence so well.

To all my siblings, dear friends, and colleagues who have supported and encouraged me through so many challenging times. I am forever grateful for how you showed up for me in the darkest moments.

To Jay, we traveled many paths in our journey as parents and I am grateful for your support and our shared life experiences. Thank you for being a loving father to our children.

As a caregiver for three decades and as a receiver of care, I have learned about the power of community and shared experiences. This journey of caregiving and healing has been challenging, but it has also been filled with moments of profound grace, gratitude, and growth. Thank you all for showing me the true meaning of love, perseverance, and the importance of self-care. May this book light the way and be a practical guide for all those navigating the beautiful, messy, world of caregiving. Remember, you are worthy of care, and your journey matters. May you find joy in your journey as you rise with resilience and move forward with purpose. With deepest gratitude and respect.

Melody Vachal

I would appreciate your feedback
on what chapters helped you most
and what you would like to see in future books.

If you enjoyed this book and found it helpful,
please leave a review on Amazon.

Visit me at
melodyvachal.com

Thank you!

www.ingramcontent.com/pod-product-compliance
Lightning Source LLC
Chambersburg PA
CBHW060526090426
42735CB00011B/2388